MR. PHILIP GUEDALLA *has also written*

ESSAYS

SUPERS AND SUPERMEN

MASTERS AND MEN

A GALLERY

HISTORY

THE SECOND EMPIRE

THE PARTITION OF EUROPE: 1715–1815

NAPOLEON AND PALESTINE: A LECTURE

FATHERS OF THE REVOLUTION

PALMERSTON

FATHERS OF THE
REVOLUTION

FATHERS OF THE REVOLUTION

BY

PHILIP GUEDALLA

"*What* an admirable place for a Declaration
of something!"—THE AMERICAN SCENE.

WITH 12 PORTRAITS

G. P. Putnam's Sons
New York & London
The Knickerbocker Press

Made in the United States of America

Dear H. G.

So much in the pages that follow was written within sight of your chimneys. So much more in the thought and writing of most persons now living lies in the shadow of something that you have already written or thought. For both reasons I want, friendship apart, to write your name in front of this book. May I?

P. G.

H. G. WELLS, Esq.

ARGUMENT

Five generations ago the United States leapt from the trap-door of history. This startling event was achieved by some men and in spite of others. Repeatedly portrayed, they somehow fail to stand vividly in the world's memory; for they were mainly presented in the stiff convention of official portraiture, which is not easily remembered; and in many cases repetition has deprived the portrait of all meaning. These studies may perform, as aids to memory, the modest duties of the sketchbook. Since they make no pretence of completeness or finality, they can have little claim to hang in the main gallery. That is reserved for life-size portraits with memorial inscriptions and rich gilding round them. But although they demand a lighter frame, they are not exercises in that tittering denigration, in which our age so frequently asserts its own superiority. Drawn with care, they may sometimes catch the turn of a head; closely rendered, they may even recall the tone of a voice. For the business of historians is, after all, the recovery of the past; and one may catch something of it in the swift movement of a lightly pencilled sketch.

CONTENTS

ILLUSTRATIONS

A SHORT TREATISE ON TRUTH

1

A SHORT TREATISE ON TRUTH

THE world (it is a proud reflection) is governed by *homo sapiens:* perhaps malicious quadrupeds, aware of our present situation, would add that it looks it. But it is not always easy to distinguish the master of the world from the remainder of the brute creation. His physical equipment is scandalously simian; and his mental qualities vary between the bovine and the bird-like. The proud attempt is often made to found a claim to superiority upon his manufactures; but even here his case is sometimes less than thin. He makes tunnels; but so does the mole. He makes bridges; but so does the beaver. He makes laws; but so (without professional assistance) does the ant. He makes filigree; but the spider makes it too. He makes songs; but the birds make better ones.

Yet there is one handicraft which is his peculiar secret. Perhaps it may serve as the mystery of the human guild. What other animal makes gods? One puts the question a little proudly and pauses, with easy confidence, for a reply. The brute creation is shamed into a respectful silence. It hangs its head:

3

its tail is (where possible) between its legs. There is no answer to the human challenge, because man alone makes gods. He makes them on the oddest occasions and from the most unpromising material. From rainstorms, from sunsets, from trees, from thunder, from running water and stones with peculiar shapes the strange little creature fashions divinities. His capacity for adoration is inexhaustible; and it is lavished upon the most remarkable objects.

But of all the gods which man has ever made the most singular are those which he makes out of other men. Sometimes the venerated person has a religious turn; in such cases he is added, quite simply, to the bright company of the skies and becomes a god *pur sang*—like the gaunt Mahomet and the mild Gautama Buddha. But more frequently his career has a merely national significance; and the deification of these political figures has produced a queer series of patriotic sub-religions which, fascinating as folk-lore, strangely complicate the task of the historian. Patriotism and centenaries are the two greatest enemies of Truth. The shy lady seems to retire into the cool depths of her well, when she hears a brass band coming or detects the deeper note of memorial orators tuning up. But she is nowhere harder to discern than in those careers which have been overlaid by this odd craving for mythology. A persevering mon-

4

arch of Teutonic origin, named Karl, reappears in
French fable as a semi-divine old man of colossal
stature, with miraculous accomplishments and in
direct communication with heaven through the Archangel Gabriel. The French imagination seems peculiarly friendly to these transfigurations. For a still
more questionable character, whom a series of happy
accidents elevated to the throne of France in the early
years of the Nineteenth Century, emerges in a blaze
of theological glory, which can hardly be stated except
in the decorous terms of classical mythology. The
fortunate artillerist

> Assumes the god,
> Affects to nod,
> And seems to shake the spheres.

A far-shining figure is seen above the thunder on the
Napoleonic Olympus; on his right hand sits the
eagle (how fortunate that his heraldic advisers did
not adopt, as they nearly did, the elephant); beside
him sits one or other of the two unhappy ladies who
were cast to play the part of Juno; and to right and
left gleams the bright circle of the lesser gods, with a
distinct preponderance of Mars and a brisk competi-
tion between his full-blooded sisters for the agreeable
rôle of Venus. Can it be wondered that historians
have failed to render the lineaments of the deified

5

Emperor? Folk-lore defies the search for truth; and any age, which has once glowed under its magic touch, is lost to history.

No period, perhaps, is richer in such mythology than the decade which produced the American Revolution. A century of patriotism has transfigured the facts; and there is a fine profusion of semi-divine personages. Infernal deities abound in Dantesque abundance. The mild features of King George III acquire, as they preside over the Brocken of British policy, a Tartaric magnificence. Lord North,

> One next himself in power, and next in crime,

shambles a little inadequately through the part of Beelzebub. And the assembled "Thrones, Dominations, Princedoms, Virtues, Powers," which lived upon the British taxpayer between the years 1760 and 1782 loom in the sinister glare of their infernal characters. One had almost forgotten that they were human beings who played at loo and lived in a pleasant world, where fine ladies said "Pho" and sent little notes to gentlemen by their abigails.

Almost equally baffling is the blinding white radiance which envelops, to the American eye, the fathers of his country. Yet Dr. Franklin was a man; General Washington was almost human; and the fatal bullet which struck down Mr. Hamilton was not averted, as it sped from Mr. Burr's pistol, by some divine mother, invisible in a cloud. One even doubts how far these laborious apotheoses perform any real service to the reputations which they are designed to glorify. One may conceivably worship, but one can never admire, a god. The adored object is removed into a sphere beyond the reach of mere affection, where his appetites are starved upon a perpetually unsatisfying diet of rather perfunctory incense. Yet these men were once alive. Those chilly figures, in their marble attitudes, had wives and doubts and failings. Each of them, after his fashion, was strong, weak, admirable, reprehensible, before a sacerdotal view of history froze him into perfection, set him in his niche, and erected him as the immobile totem of some national virtue.

And there is another side to it all. Every religion breeds its sceptics. Canonisation creates the agnostic; and great names, which might have earned respect on the human plane, become the targets of young unbelievers. Nothing is more distressing than to observe the disproportionate fall which follows overvaluation. One has seen it in innumerable poets. The popular painter waits for posterity, as for a hangman. And the same monotonous pendulum, which swings national heroes to the skies, will one day drop them almost out of sight. Did not a minor poet in New York say of a highly questionable prince, so early as the year 1837, that he was "a rather dull man of the order of Washington"? There is a stupid alternation of praise and blame; little men run about among the national images looking for feet of clay, or laboriously bleach historical black sheep. It is a singularly aimless process; and there is no corrective, except the substitution of a clear-eyed estimate for the ecstasies of patriotic religion.

Not, be it said, that all the fixed ideas are upon one side of the Atlantic. There is an equally distorted body of doctrine through which the American Revolution is reflected in the English mind. The stern figures, before which awed worshippers swing republican censers, recur in the British legend under a strange disguise. There they are oddly shrunken; they dwindle into a provincial pettiness; and their voices monotonously intone the dreary formulæ of sedition. The British misconception relates principally to the American leaders: for Englishmen have few illusions about their own. Their national modesty is rarely recognised abroad; but, by an admirable tradition, they hardly ever make extravagant claims on behalf of their public men. Profoundly respectful of themselves, they are generally economical of respect for their masters. So one is not confronted with a national cult for King George III; reference to

Mr. Grenville is rare in public speeches; and Lord
North is one of the few Tory statesmen after whom
no club in Oxford has yet been named. But in place
of the men who opposed them they have erected a
disfiguring mythology, which renders almost as little
of the facts as the loftiest flights of republican eloquence. General Washington, that profoundly British country gentleman, has become a dangerous
revolutionary; the benevolent Dr. Franklin flits
across the stage as a sinister conspirator; and Mr.
Hamilton reappears in the uncongenial character of
a dreary prig. It is all as remote from the truth as
that glorious charade which has delighted American
minds for a century with the elevating spectacle of
Lord North in the sombre trappings of Alva and the
Neronic despotism of King George.

The two myths form a pleasing contrast and may
well engage the attention of folk-lorists. Some unborn Frazer should pursue a *Golden Bough* through
the dark forest of Thanksgiving Day oratory and
Anglo-American school text-books. But the figures
of that age have surely receded far enough into the
long perspective of history for a more detached view.
Whilst they still remained relevant to public con-
troversies, politics demanded a lively distortion. The
long story was simplified into a party cry; and the
actors in the piece were plainly divided into villains

9

and heroes with a precision which brought them within the comprehension of the humblest politician. Pens were prepared for sheep and goats; and the whole diverse flock was driven in. That has been the fate of almost every great event in history. A century ago the British schoolboy approached the execution of Charles I with grave partisanship; half a century later professors exchanged challenges about the Reformation. But as Prerogative and Protestantism passed out of active politics into history, it became possible to discern the outline of the facts through a clearer (though frostier) atmosphere. So, one may hope, the American Revolution emerges slowly into the daylight. The Sons of Liberty follow the Roundheads into historic reality. Stiff figures step off their pedestals and become human once more; and men, whom one had seen fitfully under the shifting glare of patriotic limelight, sit to historians for their portraits by the still light of studios. The political controversy has almost fallen silent. The Stamp Act is no longer debated in the remoter villages of either country; and the competing eloquence of Mr. Burke and Mr. Henry compels few cheers beyond the silent applause of students in libraries. The dispute has become an old problem in administration, almost in geography; and there are no longer any sides to it, except the two sides of the Atlantic.

The debate is ended; and historians hover over that quiet battlefield.

In this still air one may set up an easel to paint a few portraits. It would be safer, perhaps, to make the usual genuflexions before the stiff effigies erected by tradition as patriotic totems. National *tabus* are awkward things to disregard. But it seems more respectful to a man, even if he was a great man, to depict him as a man. And since they lived in the hard, bright light of the Eighteenth Century, by which Mr. Walpole saw everything and M. de Voltaire saw through everything, when anxious ladies were closeted with their mantua-makers and young gentlemen of fashion eloped with pretty nymphs, how clearly one can see them, those men who (some of them without intending it) made two nations grow where one nation grew before.

H. M. KING GEORGE III

Si fractus illabatur orbis,
Impavidum ferient ruinæ.

HORACE.

H. M. KING GEORGE III

IT was a cold February night in 1820; and from the black meadows by Eton they could see lights moving in the Castle. From the park, where the trumpeters stood in the darkness, the dismal note of horns rose on the night mist; and the Yeomen of the Guard, all in black, loomed "like black giants" through the half light of a room all hung with black. In a room beyond, the King of England lay dead; and anxious heralds were forming up a long procession of solemn gentlemen by candle-light. The King was dead; and in the darkness at Windsor they were burying the poor mad old man who, for nearly twenty years, had been King Lear without Goneril, without Regan, without Cordelia. The long round of imaginary ceremonials, of unreal reviews passed with royal dignity, of illusory Parliaments opened with royal affability, was over at last; and this strange replica of one of Blake's long-bearded allegories was still. The conqueror, the captor of Napoleon; the father of the Arts and Sciences; the royal person of whom the most sonorous of his subjects observed, after a conversa-

15

tion in the library at the Queen's House in St. James's Park, "Sir, they may talk of the King as they will; but he is the finest gentleman I have ever seen"; the master of Lord Chatham, of Lord North, of Mr. Pitt; the pupil of Lord Bute; the sovereign of Garrick and Siddons and Sir Joshua and Mr. Wesley and Mr. Burke; all this and more lay in the silent room beyond the tall Yeomen in their black. For on that winter night in 1820 they were burying the Eighteenth Century.

I

It all seemed so far away. The sun shone in St. James's and Sir Robert Walpole was minister, when the Prince was born in a great house at the corner of the Square. Gin was the leading recreation and Captain Macheath the favourite character of the people of England; the sad, tinkling melodies of Miss Lockit and Miss Peachum were barely five years old, and the Italian singers had driven Handel into bankruptcy. Young Mr. Walpole was making the most of the Grand Tour, "very glad that I see Rome while it yet exists"; and little Mr. Pope was exasperating his contemporaries, whilst the outraged delicacy of Mr. Hogarth retorted in emphatic caricature. At Norfolk House the Princess of Wales lay beside a rather puny infant in the morning light. Anxious

16

George III, 1773

From an engraving in the British Museum by R. Laurie after the picture by Zoffany

ladies scurried about the house; and her Frederick, unconscious of the impending tennis-ball, looked on with large, indifferent eyes. Someone rode off to the King with the news; and outside in the Square the tiny lake gleamed in the June sunshine of 1738.

With a kind provision for its soul's welfare and a sad feeling of its approaching end, they baptised the little creature before night. But it survived them all, survived the century, even survived itself. That hurried morning and that sudden baptism were the strange opening of George's eighty years. A bishop called on the next day and gave him a string of royal names; the Poet Laureate, visited by his punctual Muse, improved the occasion in a smooth copy of heroic couplets, which contained a happy, though hardly an unexpected, allusion to Ascanius; and the infant in St. James's Square was fairly launched upon his long career of royalty.

The surroundings, it must be confessed, were not inspiring. A house in a London square without even a sentry at the door may be an apt school of simplicity. But for the other graces there was a sad dearth of instructors. The happy father, absorbed in the rather clumsy frolics to which the House of Hanover is lamentably apt in its deviations from propriety, was a rare visitor in the nursery; although he once took the child to a concert at the Foundling Hospital.

17

Yet this dismal figure, whose heavy eyes stare aimlessly out of history, was strangely popular. Nothing endears their rulers to the people of England so much as the extremes of raffishness and respectability; and Frederick's claims upon the former count were singularly high. Alike by the scale of his debts and the range of his affections he stormed the popular heart. But possibly his absence from his son may be counted for a gain to George, since Frederick was unlikely to form the young mind; although he once composed an ode in French, and cherished an obscure ambition to become Chancellor of Cambridge University on the strength, perhaps, of a silver cup which he had offered to be rowed for in a boat race. But before the boy had turned thirteen, his father was removed. A fickle nation observed without discomposure that it was "only Fred"; and graduates of either University pursued him to the sky with dirges in all the learned languages. His royal grandfather was little beyond a distant vision of an alarming old gentleman with staring eyes and a large wig, who interrupted the child with boisterous noises at an investiture of the Garter and quite frightened out of his head the little speech which he had got by heart. Nothing remained for George to lean on but his mother. She was a patient lady, who had endured without complaint her introduction into a family which exhibited most of the filial imperfections of the Atreidæ without their more pleasing features; and there was that "quiet sense" which she had brought with her from Saxe-Gotha to St. James's Square.

Two Earls, two bishops, and two gentlemen of mathematical attainments were enlisted to perfect the young intelligence, but with uneven success. The bishops did their work *à merveille* and produced a sound young Churchman. The Earls imparted whatever of peculiar attainment is in Earls. But the two scholars were a lamentable failure; and in his education George hardly reached the modest standard of a squire's son at a country grammar-school. His ignorance even became noticeable to himself in later years; and his tastes, in an age of taste, were non-existent. To this meagre curriculum his mother made two contributions, a distaste for society and the third Earl of Bute. Perhaps the first was almost natural in her. The poor lady had small cause to love the world; and she taught her son to avoid the bright and crowded assemblies, where he might, perhaps, have learnt by candle-light many lessons upon the management of men. So he remained always queer and a little lonely.

But Lord Bute was a more considerable ingredient in George's education. This accomplished person drifts into English history in a shower of rain, which stopped a cricket match near Richmond and drove the Prince's father to the dismal expedient of whist in a tent. Bute made a fourth at the card-table. His manners pleased; he called at Kew; and when he came to Court, he was attached to Frederick's Household. The Fates propelled the dreadful tennis-ball; and his master died, as he had lived, with bad French on his lips. But Bute remained beside the widow; and when her son was training to be King of England, she turned often to the graceful Scotchman. He was a man of taste; he had a leg, collected drawings, and patronised the Society of Scottish Antiquaries. His proximity to the bereaved Princess invited scandal; but he had the sense to face it. He was no fool, but merely (both by race and by conviction) a Tory. Slow to convince, the Scotch are still slower to abandon a conviction which they have once reached by the painful processes of logic; and having absorbed with difficulty the royal doctrines of the Seventeenth Century, they still adhered to the creed in 1745. Perhaps the Prince's training owed a tinge of absolutism to Bute's direction. The comforting logic with which Jacobite writers excused the errors of the Stuarts could be adapted without undue strain to the House of Hanover; and it is not surprising that a startled bishop once came upon the boy reading a Jesuit's vindication of King James II. Such studies

were unlikely to incline him to resign the throne in
favour of Charles Edward (since even Princes are
human); but they might prove a useful repertory of
ideas, should he incline to revive the glories of the
royal Prerogative. This tendency owed something
also to his mother's guidance. Reared in a German
Court where royalty had its due weight, she was
pardonably shocked by the British system which confined the Lord's anointed to making stiff bows at a
Levée, whilst the nation was administered by uncon-
secrated Whigs. This feeling, with a mother's pride,
insisted that her son should "be a King"; and there
can be small doubt that Bute showed the way. What
else he taught the Prince is tolerably obscure. A
tepid interest in medals, which Mr. Walpole once
urged Sir Horace Mann to buy for him in Tuscany,
and a total ignorance of law (imbibed from early study
of Chief Justice Blackstone's *Commentaries* in manu-
script) appear to be the only traces.

So the boy grew up; whilst the young men hunted
Sir Robert Walpole out of office, and Mr. Pitt propelled his cheering countrymen through the great
round of victories. He was a trifle solitary, "shut up
in a room," playing at Comet (but for diminutive
stakes) with the family, or living among his mother's
plants at Kew. These mild pursuits exasperated his
virile grandfather. The hero of Dettingen learned

with disgust of a royal visit to a tapestry factory. "Damn," he exclaimed, "dat tapestry—I shall have de Princes made women of." A repetition of the offence evoked reprisals: he had "oder dings to show dem dan needles and dreads," and promptly took off a small Princess to a military review in Hyde Park. He was irked by the rather Methodist virtues of his heir, who seemed "good for nothing but to read the Bible to his mother." But when he proposed to the Prince of Wales a marriage of the usual pattern with a princess from Brunswick, the mild young man refused; and Mr. Walpole was in transports over his reluctance to be "*bewolfenbuttled*, a word which I do not pretend to understand, as it is not in Mr. Johnson's new *Dictionary*." George's prejudice was personal rather than patriotic; since it appeared that he had no objection to the daughter of a German prince, upon whose territory "some frow," as Mr. Walpole said, "may have emptied her pail and drowned his dominions." For he boldly made application for the portrait of a rival beauty, who resided in the more favoured region of Saxe-Gotha. Perhaps his mother, who valued her own position as "the Lady Dowager Prudence," discouraged the Brunswick match. Perhaps (who knows?) he had a will of his own. No one could say, since the world knew little of him. And how little he knew of the world!

His travels, in the age of the Grand Tour, took him no further than Cheltenham, with one wild excursion (in delicious *incognito*) to the south of Scotland. His studies kindled little beyond a mild taste for agriculture; though he betrayed that faint inclination towards mechanics which often haunts those whose livelihood is not dependent upon their skill. He once designed a watch of tiny proportions, "rather less than a silver twopence"; but the execution was wisely left in other hands, his own mechanical achievements being almost entirely confined to turning upon a lathe, with which he was positively believed to have made a button. As a little boy he had walked through the town at night with his father

> To look at garters black and white
> On legs of female rabble.

But in spite of this initiation he never figured in the raffish world, where it was the lofty ambition of young gentlemen

> To run a horse, to make a match,
> To revel deep, to roar a catch;
> To knock a tottering watchman down,
> To sweat a woman of the town.

Indeed, he was scarcely seen in those more elegant quarters where Mr. Selwyn paraded his wit and the hackney-chairs lined up outside assemblies. One catches a glimpse of him at Miss Chudleigh's party for his birthday, when she opened the dance with the Duke of York and the court was illuminated with "a battlement of lamps." There were "pyramids and troughs of strawberries and cherries" for supper, which covered all the sideboards and even filled the chairs, although the party from the Spanish Embassy supped off fish for their conscience' sake; and the gamblers played upstairs in a long room full of bookcases, "with the finest Indian pictures on different colours and with Chinese chairs of the same colours." But he was a rare visitor; and the world knew little of him.

Yet there was so little to know. If not to be a bad man is to be a good man, George was a good man. Indeed, the private virtues consist so largely of abstention that, on the private side, his negative equipment suffices to render him quite blameless. He was a dutiful son, a faithful husband, and a devoted parent, "revered," in the pleasant terms applied to another squire, "by his family, honoured by his tenants, and awful to his domestics." But such innocuous epitaphs rarely suffice for kings. Public figures are judged by more exacting tests; and in the sphere of politics George owed his failure (for he failed) to those more positive qualities which he did not possess.

II

At twenty-two, this paragon of somewhat negative virtues became King of England. The season, in 1760, was singularly apt for his accession; and his subjects seemed to demand of him precisely what the mild young man could offer. Two revolutions and two elderly German kings had developed a new convention of the Constitution. The sovereign was no longer required to govern England. That anxious business had been transferred to a committee of his subjects, partly because, unlike the last two monarchs, they understood the English language, and partly because they were the political heirs of the men who had deposed James II and decapitated Charles I. This readjustment of responsibilities, which found a succession to the Protectorate of Oliver Cromwell in the virtual Premiership of Sir Robert Walpole and Mr. Pitt, seemed to mark the end of effective monarchy in England. The Cabinet had replaced the throne; and the sovereign, at the death of George II, had become a costly (if not particularly decorative) dignitary with purely ceremonial functions. The Birthday, the Levée, the Drawing-room were his occasions; and he was expected to perform these exacting duties, moving with due solemnity through a respectful forest of white wands and gold sticks. He might even add a military touch from time to time with a review or so, or give a bright example of royal condescension with an occasional act of charity in the more benevolent modern taste. But his main, his foremost duty was to smile and, at the appropriate moment, to incline his head. The King, in a word, had dwindled into royalty.

George was designed by Providence to play this amiable part. His physical equipment was sufficient, and the mental strain was not severe. His deportment satisfied the exacting standards of his age. He sat his throne, "graceful and genteel"; he read quite distinctly little speeches composed by other people; and in the Circle he "walks about and speaks to everybody" instead of standing, as a courtier wrote with a graceful reminiscence of his predecessor, "in one place, with his eyes fixed royally on the ground, and dropping bits of German news." The prevalent refinement seemed to have refined the coarse art of kingship into a sort of minuet. It was almost a dancing-master's business; and the formal movements, the royal airs and graces, and the ritual acts were well within George's range.

But some unhappy prompting set him a larger task. The middle years of the Eighteenth Century witnessed in almost every part of Europe a queer, belated revival of monarchy. Its inspiration came, perhaps, from the splendid pageant of autocracy through which the *Grand Monarque* had walked at Versailles. The gilt, the marble, the long perspective of respectful courtiers had stirred the envy of half the kings in Europe; and their emulation gave a sharp tilt to the falling scale of royal authority. The Seventeenth Century had been an age of great ministers; but the succeeding generation saw the kings assert themselves once more. They built great palaces and enamelled the ceilings with vast, impending goddesses; they ruled solemn vistas through the formal verdure of state gardens, with "pyramidal yews, *treillages,* and square cradle walks, with windows clipped in them"; and, stranger still, they resumed the government of their astonished countries. All Prussia was a rapier in the steady hand of Frederick; Austrian policy followed the changing moods of the Empress; and far to the north a stout, jewelled lady controlled the slow advance of Russia. Even in Spain there was a brisk revival of authority; and the scared Portuguese were bullied into progress by Pombal, as the new, glaring streets of Lisbon rose slowly in the sunshine from the dust of the earthquake. So George was in the mode when he resolved to be a King.

This project was almost the sole fruit of his meagre education. He had learned no law from Blackstone; but Lord Bute and the Jacobite pamphlets taught him a stranger lesson. George learned that he should be a King: it was his tragedy that no one taught him how to be one. His furtive study of high Stuart doctrine impressed the slow mind; ill-equipped persons are frequently consoled for their inadequacy by a belief in their sacred mission. If King James had been right (and his early reading taught George to think so), the Lord's anointed must surely be something more than a graceful gesture in a gilt chair, or an obliging signature on official sheepskins. And if, under the Whig dispensation, the royal function had almost come to that, then the Whigs must be wrong. So George, in his effort to be a King, turned Tory. There was, indeed, a Tory pattern of kingship ready to hand. The conduct of an ideal Tory on the throne had been foretold by the strange fancy of Bolingbroke; and George stumbled hopefully into the steps prescribed by that agile person for his *Patriot King*.

Defeated parties are frequently unanimous upon the impropriety of party government. Minorities are always apt to be stern critics of popular folly; and Tory thought, in the first years of Whig domination, harped on the vice of faction. But its main obsession was still the sanctity of kingship; and Bolingbroke, when he reeled back defeated from the hopeless task of imparting ideas to the exiled Stuarts and resumed the less exacting functions of a Tory oracle, blended the two notions into a strange amalgam. His friends were out of place; but he refreshed them with an odd vision of office. A new sort of monarch was to "espouse no party . . . but govern like the common father of his people." This chimera "must begin to govern as soon as he begins to reign"; and to achieve his purpose he will "call into the administration such men as he can assure himself will serve on the same principles on which he intends to govern." Such men, since the Whigs were unlikely bedfellows for an autocrat, must clearly be Tories; and in this happy dream, the dejected friends of Bolingbroke would march back into office behind the triumphant banner of "the most popular man in his country and a patriot king at the head of a united people." The bright vision faded; and in the grey light Sir Robert Walpole was ruling England for the Whig families and the German king, whom they had brought from Hanover. Even when Mr. Pitt controlled the nation, he preferred to lean on a Whig duke. So George, who wished to be King above all parties, found party in the ascendant on his coming in.

This queer young man, whom no one knew, set out to transform the government of his country; and, to a strange degree, he was successful. The odds were remarkable. The King's resources were his slender personal equipment, the vague prestige of a new reign, his mother's guidance, and the friendship of a Scotch Earl. With singular courage (and courage never failed him) he gathered these slight forces for an attack on the Whig system. A more intelligent man, one feels, would have discarded the attempt as hopeless. But George's nerve was unimpeded by sagacity; and he succeeded. The Whig façade in 1760 was impressive; Whiggery was entrenched in Parliament behind the serried rows of Newcastle's placemen; and its chosen minister, Mr. Pitt, was conquering half the world. "Two victories every week" formed an inspiring diet for civilians; and a cheering town responded with huzzas and fireworks, whilst the distant boom of the Park guns answered the salvoes from the Tower. The world observed Lord Bute at the King's elbow and made little jokes about Pitt-coal, Newcastle-coal or (hateful alternative) Scotch-coal. The King alarmed opinion with an announcement that he gloried "in the name of Briton," which sounds to posterity a brave denial of his German origins; but for contemporaries it had the more sinister ring of an admission that Scotland was in his thoughts. There was a Scotch Earl on the back stairs; and the town was not averse to little stories about "the Signora-Madre." Then, on the full tide of victory, Mr. Pitt was adroitly parted from the Whigs. His Olympian air prepared the way.

That eye, that hooked, commanding nose, which awed the House of Commons, were merely intolerable in council. For almost six years he had monopolised the control of war and foreign affairs; and British armies followed British fleets to victory in three continents. But infallible pontiffs are rarely popular with their colleagues. An issue (upon which he was plainly right) was raised in Cabinet. The oracle spoke; but the priests refused to listen. He was exasperated into resignation; and when the Whigs lost Mr. Pitt, they forfeited their sole claim to popular esteem. The oracle retired to Bath; and as the priests sat on in the temple, the outer courts were slowly emptying.

The King had made his breach in the walls of the Whig system, and the Scotch Earl became his minister. Whiggery trailed sadly into Opposition or assumed the new livery. The King, like all opponents of the party system, recruited a new party briskly. Its principles were obscure; but its advantages, since the King's Friends were grouped conveniently round the fountain of honour, were obvious. The opinions of the House of Commons were governed through its appetite for places; and Masters of the Buckhounds followed Admirals of the Red into the lobby, whilst Comptrollers of the Green Cloth, Rangers of St. James's Park, and Verdurers of Which-

31

wood Forest abandoned their absorbing duties in order to support Government in the congenial company of Lords of the Bedchamber and Governors of the Isle of Wight. For nine years the King worked steadily to impose his system. Sometimes he seemed to reach the goal, and his proud mother cried: "Now my son *is* King of England." Sometimes the dark forces of Whiggery returned upon him in the dreary form of George Grenville or the blameless incarnation of Lord Rockingham. Once there was a queer resurrection of Mr. Pitt; but he was hastily reburied under the dignity of Lord Chatham, and the patient King went on. It was a strange struggle; and it was waged against an even stranger background.

England, in the ten years between the accession of George III and the ministry of Lord North, was an odd blend of hysteria and decorum. The poets scanned; the magazines abounded in formal eloquence; and taverns echoed with the sonorous antiphonies of Johnson. The great world solemnly pursued the grave inanities of the Eighteenth Century. It dressed its hair; it played at ombre; it sat sedately through interminable plays. Mr. Walpole, up to the knees in shavings, fortified his home with gingerbread breastworks and asked the town to view the battlements, or pelted Sir Horace with commissions to buy up half the brocadella in Florence for his hangings. But beyond this decorous scene something was stirring. An odd ferment seemed to threaten the trim dignity of the age. Excited gentlemen defied propriety in hell-fire clubs; and less select assemblies grew strangely violent. There had been queer frenzies earlier in the century, when Sacheverell drove through the roaring streets, and later when half the world ran mad on stock-jobbing. But the crowds (even Mr. Walpole called it "the century of crowds") seemed madder than ever in the new reign. At first they stood to watch the little Queen come in, then stared at a Coronation, and mobbed the streets between-whiles to huzza for Pitt and Martinico or the Havannah. But their pleasant tumult dropped sharply to a deeper note as the town was swept by an odd fever; and astonished Liberty beheld the strange apostolate of Mr. Wilkes.

This indecorous, cross-eyed figure became an emblem of popular disorder upon one of those points of law by which the passionate interest of Englishmen is sometimes engaged. His private tastes lay in a simpler direction and had inspired him with an ambition to represent his country in the matrimonially congenial atmosphere of Constantinople. Failing of this, he declined in disappointment upon popular journalism and abused the Court with gusto. Involved in a welter of duels and litigation, his name became an excuse for unlimited mobbing. The tumult deepened; and for a few years the London streets were a vulgar replica of Rome in the crowded, angry days of the dying Republic, when Milo's *bravi* fought with Clodius. Bute was scared out of public life, or effaced himself to save his master; but the King persisted. It was apparently no part of the duty of a *Patriot King* to be popular; and he faced the mobs without flinching. For he had always courage. Then, gradually, the tide of disorder ebbed. The voice of authority became faintly audible above the sound of breaking glass; and when it came, it spoke in the King's name. The Whigs were quite subdued now; and England was governed by George himself through a peering, pouting minister with "the air of a blind trumpeter." It was the year 1770, and Lord North was waiting sedately in the wings.

III

Personal government depends for its success upon two factors, the person and the governed. When a rare conjunction unites administrative talent with a docile or a sympathetic people, the world is presented with the strange miracle of successful autocracy. But how rare such unions are. Capacity, infrequent among statesmen, is still less frequent among kings; and docility, west of the Vistula, has been extinct among subjects for almost three centuries. A national impulse rarely coincides with a monarch's wishes. The case, of course, is not unknown; the laborious versatility of Frederick might drive an obedient Prussia, and the universal competence of Napoleon found its true partner in the French energy released by a national revolution. But these are the rare triumphs of monarchy. More often, far more often, a distracted autocrat fumbles with his work; or a nation, disinclined to play its humble part, renders it impossible. If the ruler is unequal to his high position, autocracy fails. If his subjects withhold consent to his wide authority, it fails as gravely. The sole possibility of success for personal government lies in the combination of an adequate person with a consenting people; and its failures, for lack of that rare conjunction, are more numerous than its successes.

The King's experiment was sadly deficient in both elements. Viewed as a candidate for autocracy, George was singularly unimpressive; even Bolingbroke, one feels, would have been discouraged by the spectacle of his *Patriot King* in action. The patient, punctual creature minuting his correspondence with the hour of despatch; directing at "2 min. pt. 11 a.m." the march of some cavalry from Henley to Hounslow; consenting at "53 min. pt. 5 p.m." to the appointment of a Mr. Fountayne to the living of Worples-

don; complaining at "12 min. pt. 10 p.m." that if
James Adam is appointed Surveyor-General to the
Board of Works, he "shall certainly think it hard on
Chambers, and shall in that case only think he must
not be passed by"; insisting at "57 min. pt. 11 a.m."
that the new prebendary of Durham must "continue
to attend the young Chancellor"; this plodding figure,
stooping over his green box in the candle-light and
holding the papers close to his face before he traced
the big G.R., seems so remote from the high dream of
kingship. "The common father of his people . . ."
and a light burning late in the Queen's House, where
an angry man was writing little hints to the Common
Council for unseating Mr. Alderman Wilkes. "The
most popular man in his country . . ." noting gentlemen of the House of Commons to receive a frown at
the Levée for an injudicious vote. "A patriot king
at the head of a united people . . ." pelting a driven
Minister with little punctual notes. How far they
seem, those busy, irritable little figures, below that
imagined monarch who was to sit enthroned above
the clouds of party and bathed in the pure sunlight
of autocracy. His teachers had urged him to be a
King; and someone, it seemed, had taught him to be
a passable Patronage Secretary. Clerks in his Treasury formed such habits; industrious merchants sought
vainly to impart them to their sons; and his intellec-

tual counterparts crouched on tall stools in counting-houses east of Temple Bar.

Yet he was not content to drug himself with the deadly narcotic of administrative detail. For he was King; and policy, as well as patronage, claimed the royal attention. Patronage was his forte, and it served well enough as a solvent of most domestic problems. He set about to govern England single-handed. Now, there was a House of Commons to be perpetually shielded from unwholesome influences, and George went in pursuit of political purity down unusual paths. The minor disorder of elections was cured with "gold pills"; and the tiresome scruples of elected persons yielded on most occasions to a gracious nod from the throne and a word behind Lord North's hand, followed after a becoming interval by a line in the *London Gazette* and a precious package from the Pay Office on quarter-day. The King, by this simple artifice, was his own First Minister and Chief Whip. His deputy sat dozing in the House of Commons, ran errands for his master, and stoutly maintained that the office of Prime Minister was unknown to the Constitution. The King had formed a party, led it, satisfied its simple needs, and maintained it in office. To that extent his experiment in personal government was verging towards success at home. The Whigs were helpless; since Parliament was for the King, and they professed to believe in government by Parliament. They roared in debate; they brought down votes "in flannels and blankets, till the floor of the House looked like the pool of Bethesda." But they were outvoted and retired to mutter in the deep libraries of country houses. Nothing seemed to remain in opposition except the City and the mob. But the Mansion House, strange temple of democracy, was a mere nest of preposterous Aldermen; and if the mob stirred, there were still the Guards.

George governed England with an odd blend of force and persuasion; and his subjects seemed curiously content to acquiesce. He had made peace; and great liberties are permitted to statesmen who make peace. He had unseated Mr. Pitt; but Mr. Pitt had made his name grotesque with a peerage. He challenged democracy; but democracy, in 1765, stood for little beyond the mob. Men had died for Hampden; but it would be fantastic to die for Mr. Wilkes. It almost seemed, at home, that it was possible to govern an empire with the arts of a Chief Whip. But one section of his people presented a queer, unyielding obstacle. Three thousand miles from the Levée, six weeks away from Lord North's significant smile, the Americans still persisted in their tedious debate. The ripe intelligence of Mr. Grenville had devised some taxes for them. Taxes, it seemed, were the common lot of victorious nations. So that imperial mind, which added the Isle of Man to the British Empire, sent stamps to Boston that inspired a strange repugnance. Mr. Grenville was frankly baffled. He had drawn the scheme (and he was at home in the schedule of a revenue Bill), because the neat device of stamps appealed irresistibly to that orderly mind. He had looked up the law (and he was a fair lawyer) and discovered the helpful precedent of the Channel Islands. Yet it was odd that mobs paraded in the clear American light and local orators abounded in deep-chested sentiments about liberty: perhaps the colour of the stamps was wrong. Then the grave leaders of the Whig groups faced the strange problem (and even Mr. Walpole began to notice that it was a "thorny point"). Mr. Grenville had thought of stamps; they thought of tea; few men in England thought of a larger issue. Then the Whigs subsided; and the King (with him, Lord North) resumed control of his bewildered empire. That he grasped the American issue is improbable. It was enough for that determined, angry man that the law of England had been defied on British territory. Wilkites in Southwark or Sons of Liberty in King Street, Boston, were the same to him; the troops must do their duty. Men who had ridden out the wild storm of the Middlesex election were not likely to parley with a mob; and at a distance of three thousand miles the solemn ratiocinations of a Boston town meeting were indistinguishable from the Brentford rabble. Even if he reflected, it was unlikely that the King would side with the colonists. Had he not learnt the sanctity of authority in a stiff Jacobite school? Passive obedience was the first duty of a loyal subject. Admirable in Great Britain, this virtue was yet more essential in America, since colonies (it was the lesson of his master Bolingbroke) were "like so many farms of the mother country." George was a farmer; and the strange claim of one of his farms to be consulted about its cultivation was clearly inadmissible.

The angry voices rose higher in the deepening tumult; and as the scattered shots rang out down the long road to Concord on a spring day in 1775, the argument drifted into civil war. The King was firm. Indeed he had already fortified his resolution with the advice of the sagacious Gage. The conversation of military men upon political topics is a rare stimulant for civilians; and that warrior had persuaded his sovereign that the Americans "will be lyons whilst we are lambs; but, if we take the resolute part, they will undoubtedly prove very meek." In this hopeful mood he flogged the Boston Port Act through Parliament and hallooed Lord North to hunt the Opposition through the lobbies. He was still "well convinced they will soon submit," as Israel Putnam drove his sheep to Boston and Colonel Washington insisted warily that it was "a folly to attempt more than we can execute." The issue looked so simple in St. James's; and as the American tone hardened, the King could only ejaculate, "The dye is now cast, the colonies must either submit or triumph." But his mood was not one of blind repression. Like all Englishmen on the verge of a practical concession, he insisted firmly on his technical rights: "I do not wish to come to severer measures, but we must not retreat; by coolness and an unremitted pursuit of the measures that have been adopted I trust they will come to submit; I have no objection afterwards to their seeing that there is no inclination for the present to lay fresh taxes on them, but I am clear there must always be one tax to keep up the right, and as such I approve of the Tea Duty." So the student of Blackstone pressed his point of law, seeking little more than an admission which might cover his retreat. How many solicitors have been instructed to threaten proceedings in that confident tone. Unhappily he knew too little of men to measure the results of his threat. The lonely boy had become a lonely man; and his solitude was increased by the still lonelier elevation of a throne. He saw his fellow-creatures down the warped perspective of a king. But some instinct might have told him that Englishmen, in Boston or in Westminster Hall, willing enough to make all practical concessions, rarely give up a point of law. That, in essence, was his own attitude in the argument; and he lacked the wit to see that other men might feel the same. He knew so little of other men; and those incalculable creatures in America remained a mystery upon the far horizon of the world.

But when his challenge was accepted, when the expected lambs declined to play their part, he entered with gusto upon the detail of the war. Provisions for the army, the loan of infantry from Hanover, a purchase of recruits in Hesse-Cassel, sea strategy, dates of embarkation, biscuit and flour, the beating orders for enlisting Campbells, Gordons, and Macdonalds, plans of campaign, and news of privateers passed rapidly under the busy pen at Kew or the Queen's House. He watched the war like an eager parent, sailed the crowded troop-ships in imagination from Hamburgh to Sandy Hook, and followed his red-coats, as the winding line of bayonets vanished into the darkness of the great trees. Dimly he saw that personal government had met the fatal challenge of an unconsenting people. He seemed to feel that he was fighting for the throne of England; because if England thought with the unhappy rebels, "I should not

esteem my situation in this country as a very digni-
fied one, for the islands would soon cast off all
obedience." It was (he saw the issue now) the
decisive struggle of authority against all the dark
forces which had ever opposed him, against the
Whigs, against the mob, against the grinning mask
of Wilkes and the sonorous tutorship of Chatham,
against Mr. Burke and his heresies and the insidious
logic of Dr. Franklin. George saw all his enemies
gathered into the head of a single rebellion, and
struck hard. The swelling strength of the Opposition
alarmed Lord North; but the King's nerve was
steady. "Whilst any ten men in the kingdom will
stand by me, I will not give myself up into bondage.
My dear Lord, I will rather risk my crown"—the
sprawling hand wrote firmly on—"than do what I
think personally disgraceful; and whilst I have no
wish but for the good and prosperity of my country,
it is impossible that the nation shall not stand by me;
if they will not, they shall have another king, for I
will never put my hand to what would make me
miserable to the last hour of my life."

The French guns chimed in, as Versailles discovered
a pleasing coincidence of romantic impulse with
national interest; and for a moment he seemed almost
to face the certainty of surrender in the revolted
colonies. But "I will never consent that in any

treaty that may be concluded a single word be mentioned concerning Canada, Nova Scotia, or the Floridas, which are colonies belonging to this country . . . for it is by them we are to keep a certain awe over the abandoned colonies." The issue had travelled far beyond taxation. In Europe it was now a war of existence with an ancient enemy; and in America it raised the vital problem of secession. That question was to haunt the continent for ninety years, and George stated it in terms which strangely anticipate the American echoes of a century later: "If Lord North can see with the same degree of enthusiasm I do the beauty, excellence, and perfection of the British constitution as by law established, and consider that, if any one branch of the empire is allowed to cast off its dependency, that the others will infallibly follow the example,"—how odd to find the thought of Lincoln in the mind of George III!— "that consequently, though an arduous struggle, that is worth going through any difficulty to preserve to latest posterity what the wisdom of our ancestors have carefully transmitted to us, he will not allow despondency to find a place in his breast, but resolve not merely out of duty to fill his post, but will resolve with vigour to meet every obstacle that may arise, he shall meet with most cordial support from me; but the times require vigour, or the state will be ruined."

That cry, half strangled by the long, tortuous sentence, is not ignoble. The tenacious man, who stumbled into war in blind resentment of disorder, had a wider vision. The King could see the issue now; and, granted the fatal difference between autocracy and republic, he saw it almost with the eyes of 1861: "I own that, let any war be ever so successful, if persons will sit down and weigh the expenses, they will find, as in the last, that it has impoverished the state, enriched individuals, and perhaps raised the name only of the conquerors; but this is only weighing such events in the scale of a tradesman behind his counter; it is necessary for those in the station it has pleased Divine Providence to place me, to weigh whether expenses, though very great, are not sometimes necessary to prevent what might be more ruinous to a country than the loss of money. The present contest with America I cannot help seeing as the most serious in which any country was ever engaged; it contains such a train of consequences that they must be examined to feel its real weight. Whether the laying of a tax was deserving all the evils that have arisen from it, I should suppose no man could allege that without being more fit for Bedlam than a seat in the Senate; but step by step the demands of America have arisen; independence is their object; that certainly is one which every man not willing to sacrifice every object to a *momentary* and inglorious peace must concur with me in thinking that this country can never submit to: should America succeed in that, the West Indies must follow them . . . Ireland would soon follow the same plan and be a separate state; then this island would be reduced to itself, and soon would be a poor island indeed . . ."

The harassed man at Kew wrote on; and three thousand miles away the guns were booming in the summer sunshine of 1779. His courage held; he searched himself with "frequent and severe self-examination." When the news was good, he prepared to show America "that the parent's heart is still affectionate to the penitent child." When it was bad, he reflected that "in this world it is not right alone to view evils, but to consider whether they can be avoided, and what means are the most efficacious." In this sturdy temper he held on, defying the Opposition, heartening the pardonably despondent North. On a July day in 1781, he was still insisting that "this long contest will end as it ought, by the colonies returning to the mother country, and I confess I will never put my hand to any other conclusion of this business." But in those hot summer weeks a tired army was trailing about Virginia behind Cornwallis. At the fall of the year they stood behind a line of battered earthworks by the York River. The French lay off the coast; and in the sloping fields beyond the little town the parallels crept slowly nearer. There was a steady roll of musketry. Then the British guns fell silent; and the war was ended.

IV

Four years later, on a dark winter afternoon Miss Burney was mildly startled by a visitor. They were playing Christmas games after dinner in Mrs. Delany's little drawing-room at Windsor, when the door opened quietly. It closed again behind "a large man in deep mourning," whom no one except Miss Burney seemed to notice. He said nothing; but as that sharp little eye travelled down the black suit, it encountered, heavens! the glitter of a star. Then one of the young ladies turned round on him, stifled a scream, and called out, "The King!—Aunt, the King!" The little company backed uneasily into the corners of the room; and presently there was a loud royal whisper of "Is that Miss Burney?" Her sovereign bowed politely; and the talk ran upon the whooping-cough, which prevailed in the royal nursery, and James's Powders, which Princess Elizabeth found so beneficial. Then he rained little questions on her; how she came to write *Evelina*, how to publish, how to print without a word to her father.

Urged by the royal *What!* she said with a simper that she had "thought it would look very well in print." The awkward questioning went on, until a rap at the door announced the Queen, and someone slid out for candles to light the ugly little lady in.

Another day the royal mind was easier. The children were off to Kew for a change of air, and James's miraculous powders had done their work; so the talk ran on books. Voltaire was "a monster—I own it fairly." Rousseau was thought of "with more favour, though by no means with approbation." And Shakespeare—"was there ever such stuff as great part of Shakespeare? Only one must not say so! But what think you?—What?—Is there not sad stuff?—What?—what?" Miss Burney temporised. But her sovereign enjoyed his little heresy and laughed. "Oh! I know it is not to be said! but it's true. Only it's Shakespeare, and nobody dare abuse him." So the arch monarch developed his wicked theme and shocked the bookish lady—"but," as the coy iconoclast confessed, "one should be stoned for saying so!"

The "fatal day" had come, bringing an end to the strange experiment of personal government. At home he dwindled by slow degrees into an almost constitutional monarch; and overseas Mr. Jay read with some surprise that when Mr. Adams made his

bow as ambassador, the King had stifled all resentment in a graceful confession—"I will be very frank
with you. I was the last to conform to the separation; but the separation having been made, and
having become inevitable, I have always said, as I
say now, that I would be the first to meet the friendship of the United States as an independent power."

This pleasant, ageing, stoutish man, with his odd,
jerky questions and his staring eyes, slowly became
a ceremonial monarch of the standard Hanoverian
pattern; displaying, on the appropriate occasions, a
becoming versatility of martial and civilian accomplishments; strolling in the evening light on the
Terrace at Windsor, surrounded by a family that was
a Court in itself; admiring Miss Burney in the famous
lilac tabby which the Queen gave her; pressing the
remedial virtues of barley-water upon an exhausted
colonel after a hard day in the hunting field; trotting,
gnawed by the incurable inquisitiveness of royalty,
into half the shops in Windsor; taking, after a more
than usually incompetent attempt on his life, "his
accustomed doze" at the theatre; peering, smiling,
bowing. This amiable, domestic, elderly person,
with his little jokes and the quick, questioning
What?—what? forms a queer postscript to the high
adventure of the young, friendless King, who set out
to govern England and lost America. It all seemed

49

so far away now. Mr. Wilkes had faded, Mr. Pitt had died in that theatrical way of his; Lord North was still living somewhere, but he was quite blind now. The King lived on, before all else a father and a husband, the Georgian head of an oddly Victorian court.

But he had still, had always his courage. It had not failed him on "Black Wednesday," when at the height of the war the mob ran wild for "No Popery" and Lord George Gordon. The streets were alight with the disordered worship of this singular idol, whose evangelical quest for a form of Christianity uncorrupted by Popish additions finally led him, by the fatal logic of a Scotsman or a lunatic, into a clear air where it was uncontaminated even by a Saviour. London passed sleepless nights and crept about behind its shutters. But the King informed his Council that, if the Riot Act was to be read before the troops could fire into the crowds, one magistrate at least would do his duty and then could take command of his Guards in person. The same even temper bore him up when a mad woman thrust a knife at him one afternoon outside the garden door at St. James's. He steadied the crowd, went in to hold his Levée, and then drove down to Windsor to show himself to the Queen. Three royal persons and two ladies in waiting mingled their tears. But the careful King enquired, "Has she cut my waistcoat? Look! for I have had no time to examine." His courage barely failed beneath the slow, dreadful gathering of a darker cloud, which hung above him. That he saw its coming is almost certain. Little doubt is left by his choking exclamation, "I wish to God I may die, for I am going to be mad." Then, staring with pitiable eyes at the ebbing tide of reason, he faded into insanity.

Once he returned; and for ten years he presided over the state where he had reigned. The Whigs were out; but England was ruled by a minister again, and Mr. Pitt—there was a new Mr. Pitt now, whose "damned long ugly face" was almost as trying as Chatham's eye—sat in his father's seat. The *Patriot King* had declined into dogeship, although there was a faint flicker of the old authority, when the minister roused his sovereign's Churchmanship with some nonsense about equality for Irish Papists. He rode; he played piquet; he bathed in the loyal waves of Weymouth. There was a pleasant jingle of Light Dragoons on the little Esplanade, and his troopers lounged in their sunny Capua beside the Wessex sea—

> When we lay where Budmouth Beach is,
> O, the girls were fresh as peaches
> With their tall and tossing figures and their eyes of blue and
> brown!

And our hearts would ache with longing
As we paced from our sing-songing,
With a smart *Clink! Clink!* up the Esplanade and down.

The bathing-women all wore "God save the King" on ample girdles round their waists; and as the royal person plunged, that pious invocation burst from the muffled fiddlers in a bathing-machine. He strolled again upon the Terrace at Windsor. But this time his airing was a martial exercise. For the French guns were speaking across Europe, and George called for the band to play "Britons, strike home." So the old man (he was rising seventy now) confronted Buonaparte. He grasped, one feels, as little of the strange forces which opposed him as of the American tangle. He did little more than clench an English fist and shake it in the face of France.

But whilst he struggled to retain the last remains of sight, his watchful frigates kept the sea; his guns rang out where the Spanish hills dip to Trafalgar, and his red-coats stared at the cactus along the dusty roads of Portugal. Then, once again, a cloud swung over the sun and his sky darkened. The war went on; there was a steady thunder of guns in Europe, until at the last they stood smoking in the sodden fields by Waterloo. But the King sat muttering in a closed room at Windsor. He was far away in a pleasant world, where he gave interminable audiences to dead

52

ministers. For hours, for days, for years he talked with them; and sometimes he made himself a little music on an old spinet, which had been silent since Queen Anne. Then he faded out of life; and on a winter night in 1820 Mr. Croker watched the mourners marshalling and heard the dismal note of horns from the Great Park.

H. M. KING LOUIS XVI

> *Dans le vieux pare solitaire et glacé,*
> *Deux spectres ont évoqué le passé.*
> COLLOQUE SENTIMENTAL.

H. M. KING LOUIS XVI

IT still hangs faintly in the air, the last, unfinished melody of the French monarchy. Thin and remote, it seems to drift among the trees at Trianon. Yet sometimes, before it wavers and dies away, one may catch it, like a band of violins busy with a brisk *rigaudon* of Philidor or some solemn concert-piece of Pergolesi. Other ages return upon us with a fuller note. Rome was a gust of trumpets across Europe; and the Church may live again in the slow thunder of an organ in a distant aisle. Islam returns in a wailing minor and a strange, regular throb of little drums. The lost empires of the East are found again in a sound of temple bells or a wild clamour of gongs. But of that time the note which still hangs upon the air is a faint throb of busy violins.

I

The King was a little dull. Perhaps the dwellers in eventful periods seem always a little dull to their sage posterity. Lamentably deficient in perspective, they are in many cases quite disgracefully unaware

57

of their own times. But it is so easy, when one has the wisdom to be born a century later, to appraise the significance of facts. They seem to fall in line, to range themselves processionally, to move off smartly at the word of command towards an inevitable destination. Those insistent drums, one feels, must surely have assailed intelligent ears; that bright banner, which led in the long column of marching circumstance, can hardly have escaped the dull contemporary eye. But to the crowds, which watched them pass, they were a disorderly and divergent throng. It filled the scene; it formed, and shifted, and melted, and formed again; and the air was full of the vague murmur of its movement. There was just (as there always is) a passing welter of events, lacking all symmetry, untuned to any dominant note, and totally unproductive of judicious reflections. This agreeable turmoil is all that contemporaries observe of grave historical events. It may, perhaps, excuse their dullness. Even ourselves, bewildered travellers in an overcrowded train of consequence, may stand one day in need of such posthumous indulgence. But, undeniably, the King was a little dull.

He was never sprightly. To Mr. Walpole, although reminded by him of a Duke, he seemed "an *imbécile* both in mind and body." The great nose jutted from a mild, lethargic face; his lips were set in the fixed

58

Louis XVI, 1789

From an engraving in the British Museum published by A. Sergent

smile of ceremony; and he was unhandy in his movements. He had stared, a weak-eyed boy, at the bright, bedizened world where his tall grandfather sat with a surprising Countess, who juggled with oranges at table. Once (but the child can hardly have been present) she threw her powder over the King and called him *Jean Farine*. The waning century was in its third quarter now; and the long round of public scenes—the shuffling crowds at Levée, the Guards, the *cordons bleus*, the staring faces, the whispering at a *lit de justice*—went slowly on in the failing sunshine. They prompted him: and he made the movements of a Dauphin, with solemn airs at mass and stiff bows for foreign gentlemen who came to Court. They prompted him again: and he stumbled through a wedding in the tall, gleaming chapel at Versailles with a fair girl beside him, who smiled and turned her head. There was a touch of thunder in the air; and when they were back again in the Château, the storm broke. The scene, the long unmeaning scene changed slowly round him. Soon he was standing with his brothers at the foot of a stair, while the King, in a stifling room beyond, muttered repentance to a Cardinal. The old man wavered and failed, and rallied, and failed again. There was a long silence in the great room. A candle was snuffed at a window, and the waiting riders spurred out into France with word that the King was dead.

Then he was King himself. More faces stared; there was an ecstasy of etiquette; and the vague eyes and the unchanging smile looked down from a throne. Sometimes he nearly seemed at ease, when his Queen went riding in the Bois, and he kissed her soundly in a cheering crowd. His air was almost royal as he stood, crowned and in ermine, amongst the candles in the great nave of Reims, whilst a tall girl beside him wept for joy and weariness, and guns and carillons and singing birds proclaimed him. But mostly he went a little heavily with slow, uncertain movements. He seemed to lumber through a world of pirouettes; and in an age of general urbanity he had a rustic air. A fine Italian gentleman found his rusticity almost Iroquois. He seemed *selvaggio*, even *rozzo* to the fastidious observer from Naples. One might almost say that he was born and bred under the sky—*nato ed educato en un bosco*—that he had learned his breeding in a wood.

II

In a wood, but a quite other wood, his lady lived. It lay, in a most elegant disorder, beyond the straight walks of the Château. That interminable perspective drove. like a knife, towards the two poplars in

the west; the trim borders parted neatly as it swept
by; and solemn alleys disclosed respectful statuary
down grave, rectangular vistas. Somewhere beyond,
a decorous avenue ended in a tiny palace of white
stone. Built, years before, for Pompadour (and paid
for, by a delicious subterfuge, under the solemn
rubric of Foreign Affairs), it still kept something of
her grace. Its slim pillars seemed to have all the
elegance which had held a tired man for twenty years;
and in the shapely windows there was, perhaps, a
memory of her fine eyes. Beyond it the little paths
wandered uncertainly among the trees. They were
disposed in the English mode, with rocks and water-
falls in calculated disarray. Plantations out of line,
streams that perpetually curved under little bridges,
a temple, and a ruin or so composed an odd, delightful blend of the *ton grec* with the *ton chinois*. And
there, among the trees, the Queen lived, *petite reine
de vingt ans* in her *Petit Vienne* as they called it.
Mr. Burke had seen her—"it is now sixteen or seventeen years since"—and his great spectacles still
gleamed at the recollection. He saw her "just above
the horizon, decorating and cheering the elevated
sphere she just began to move in—glittering like the
morning-star, full of life, and splendour, and joy."
Mr. Walpole could recall a figure "in silver, scattered
over with *laurier-roses*," seen at a *bal paré*, where

"it was impossible to see anything but the Queen. Hebes and Floras, and Helens and Graces are street-walkers to her." But that had been at Versailles. Her true life, like Louis' breeding, was in her wood—*en un bosco*—at Trianon.

M. de Caraman, that accomplished soldier, had planned it. The polite world (other than taxpayers) found it perfect. The Prince de Ligne, stern critic of horticulture, failed to detect a single fault except in a solitary parterre, which offended him by its *air un peu trop ruban;* but he adored the grotto. A lyric Abbé recited some charming couplets on the subject; and a young gentleman contributed to the *Almanach des Muses* for 1780 an elegy (subsequently reprinted in his *Amours*) which did equal credit to his sensibility and his botanical knowledge. Even the King was pleased. Stout, nervous, a little sleepy, he was rarely at ease in company. He preferred the easy contacts of the hunting-field to the grave ritual of his palaces. But he was often at Trianon. Versailles was a *corvée*, where one sat in ceremonial attitudes or wandered, for a blameless distraction, in the high attics to watch the men and horses moving like flies in the great court below. But one could go down to Trianon on a bright morning for breakfast with a smiling, high-coloured lady; sit half the day at ease in her garden, reading a book in the shade of a tall tree; sup with her, play a hand of cards, and drive back to the Château through the cool darkness.

It seemed to lie remote from the busy actual world, where M. Turgot made his economies and M. de Vergennes had his policies—those unending policies which were to regild the fading glories of Versailles. That exquisitely frowning rock, which only learned to frown correctly after fourteen models had passed the royal eye; the artless recesses of the grotto, seven times rehearsed by patient architects; the quiet pools; the streams; the little bridges; those adorable sphinxes, sedately couchant round a marble octagon, smiling eight different smiles and wearing their charming plaits in eight differing modes—one of them (how like a sphinx) à l'égyptienne—these made a world separated by exquisite distances from reality. It was a pleasant, summer world, where the light fell slanting through tall trees, while far guns boomed across the Chesapeake and woke strange echoes in French minds. Queens played at dairymaids in becoming hats, or exchanged lambs with duchesses as pledges of village friendship. Gentlemen walked at ease en frac; or fluted in bushes on fine nights, disguised as Roman shepherds, whilst the lifting note of hautboys played by two elegant satyrs kept time from an adjacent hedgerow, and a bright blaze behind the little temple outlined the god on his pedestal and gleamed in the dark lake. Sometimes (for even the actresses were unreal at Trianon) a royal lady took the lighted stage in a tiny playhouse of blue silk; to simper through the operatic virtues of *Perrette;* to present *Agathe,* the chaste laundress, ironing linen; to embroider cuffs for a stage valet, the coy offering of a stage *soubrette.* Once her sovereign, smiling in his seat and staring through the myopic haze, ventured upon a hiss. The indignant actress checked her song, swept him a curtsey and, bold as brass, retorted, *"Monsieur, si vous n'êtes pas content des artistes, allez à la porte et on vous rendra votre argent."* She took her pleasure with eager hands, as that official knew who, harassed for a trifle of furniture, once wrote to a colleague, *"Vous connaissez notre maîtresse: elle aime bien à jouir promptement."* Swiftly indeed she took her pleasure under the trees. For the leaves were falling at Trianon.

III

Sometimes reality intruded upon them. Once, when the reign was barely a year old, it came surging in through the iron gates below the Château. It flooded the great courtyard, and in the spring sunshine of 1775 it roared for bread below the palace windows. The solemn windows stared, as it thundred against the bolted doors; and the busts in the *Cour de Marbre* looked down with their blind, marble eyes. But the great palace stood silent in the sunshine. The bayonets were somewhere out of sight; and, by the King's order, there was no musketry. Then, as the Guards began to muster, he stood in one of the tall windows and spoke from a balcony. But his words died on the uproar; and as he turned away, the boy (he was just twenty) shed tears. It was a wild and testing day, and the world seemed so difficult. He faced it with heavy, tearful eyes; and as the great crowd rolled off towards Paris with the noise and movement of a refluent wave, he moved slowly about the palace.

But reality did not always visit them in such crowded and tumultuous forms. Once it was introduced in a plain suit, wearing the delicious incognito of "Count Falkenstein." He came, imperially, from Schönbrunn to see a royal sister at Versailles, and the sensibility of poets was moved to rapture by the devoted pair:

> *Dis avec moi, ma Glycère,*
> *Rien n'est si bon que le frère,*
> *Rien n'est si beau que la sœur.*

His conversation was, in the main, improving. Joseph was always a little trying. But when he spoke from the double pulpit of an elder brother and a blameless Emperor, he rose to strange heights of good advice. He alluded, in a steady flow, to the vice of extravagance, the impropriety of games of chance, and the undesirability of bad companions. He spoke, with profound emotion, of family life; nor did the prevailing mode of hairdressing pass unnoticed by his stern eye. In vain they tried distractions—Italian opera, a dinner among the trees at Trianon, a ballet, and the *Comédie Française* in a diverting piece. But actors, *corps de ballet*, cooks, and singers plied him in vain; and the relentless stream of good advice flowed on. He even found time (for Joseph was an indomitable sightseer, who was to visit in a crowded lifetime almost all his own dominions) for a few helpful words upon the sights of Paris, of which the King of France was lamentably ignorant. "*Vous possédez le plus bel édifice de l'Europe*," observed the informing visitor. His patient brother-in-law inquired a little dully, "*Lequel?*" "*Les Invalides*," was the firm reply, spoken (one feels) with assurance and a slight German accent. Louis had heard so. Shocked by his languor, Joseph pressed him further. Had the King, then, not visited this jewel of his crown? "*Ma foi non*," said the stout young man. "*Ni moi*," cried his cheerful Queen, "*non plus*." Her brother turned upon her the unvarying smile of brothers:

"Ah!" he said, *"pour vous, ma sœur, je n'en suis pas étonné, vous avez tant d'affaires."* And so in a cloud of good advice, he departed.

Late in the same year (it was 1777) a more vivid reality came to Court. For the sloop *Reprisal* had made an abominable passage of thirty days from the Delaware; and Dr. Franklin was knocking at the exquisite doors, behind which French policy lurked in the busy mind of M. de Vergennes. The Count was most obliging. For that accomplished man had already reached an intelligent conviction that "Wise and happy will that nation be which will be the first to adapt its policy to the new circumstances of the age, and to consent to see in its colonies nothing more than allied provinces and no longer subject States of the motherland." It was, perhaps, unfortunate that this enlightened view was reached too late for application to any colonies of France; because, since the last war, there were none. But it was sound philosophy; and was not philosophy *à la mode?* It might even serve a loftier end, since England, with an incurable lack of philosophy, still had colonies; and the grand experiment of liberty might well be tried *in corpore vili.* There are few more touching spectacles in history than the degree to which hostility to England reconciles foreign statesmen to the noblest causes. No quest can be too high, no crusade too quixotic, if only its prosecution conduces to the discomfiture of England. Her victims groan unheard for generations, until an enterprising rival inclines a sympathetic ear. For the cry of Ireland, the complaint of Egypt, the low call of India have always made a peculiar appeal to her enemies.

The Thirteen Colonies were not unfavourably placed, since M. de Vergennes was already proclaiming that *le moment est venu de venger les puissances maritimes de la suprématie insolente de l'Angleterre.* Such a view was not unpromising for the Colonies. His grasp of the major issue of taxation was uncertain; and perhaps the finer feelings of one who had observed without undue distress the First Partition of Poland might be a trifle blunted. But he felt no doubt of his country's attitude to England: *Il faut la faire rentrer dans l'ordre des puissances tributaires où elle a réduit la France, lui ravir l'empire qu'elle prétend exercer dans les quatre parties du monde, avec autant d'orgueil que d'injustice.* That was a conviction, by the clear light of which a man might take his way through the mazes of American policy. Nice questions of taxation, the awkward problem of belligerent recognition, points of blockade and prize, could all be solved by a simple craving for *revanche.* That it had little reference to the heroic colonists was immaterial. Their cause would serve to thrill the *salons*, to flush young ladies at Versailles with thoughts of liberty, to ship young gentlemen overseas—*braves comme leurs épées, pleins de courage, de talents, et de zèle pour notre cause*—in defence of the mysterious sanctity of representative institutions. But behind the pale gilt tracery of its exquisite doors, where the lyre, the tripod, and the sphinx were replacing the loves and bouquets of a more frivolous age, French statesmanship had other thoughts. Under Louis XV it had laughed a little wrily at defeat. But under Louis XVI it remembered bitterly the long war with Mr. Pitt, the sunken fleets and the lost colonies. A second war might revive commerce and win new sugar-islands. It might, above all, break England and regild the lilies. Had not Choiseul foreseen it, when he wrote twelve years before, *La révolution d'Amérique remettra l'Angleterre dans l'état de faiblesse où elle ne sera plus à craindre en Europe?* To miss that simple path would have required less than a man, less than a Frenchman; and when M. de Vergennes followed it, it brought him straight to the American alliance.

His royal master was advised of the course of French policy. He stared with heavy eyes at a long memorial by Vergennes, and he heard Turgot object at Council. But Turgot always objected, and Vergennes was full of reasons. So his country drifted into the last war of the French monarchy, whilst Dr. Franklin sat writing in his room at Passy, and persons of fashion cultivated the republican virtues, and Versailles watched the smoke curl slowly above the royal workshop or heard the faint echo of the King's hunting horns. His ministers, after a year of gun-running, grasped at the new alliance. There were long talks at Mr. Deane's in Paris, hasty copyings and recopyings at Passy; and at last, on a Friday, the treaties were signed. *Les insurgens* were promoted to alliance with the Most Christian King.

Then Dr. Franklin had his audience, dressed in his best. He wore no powder on his head, plain silver buckles, white stockings, and a dark suit; and Madame Campan was enraptured by this *costume d'un cultivateur américain.* Unsuited, perhaps, to agriculture, it was yet in exquisite contrast with Versailles. Simplicity had been preserved, without disrespect. The fur cap—that "martin fur cap among the powdered heads of Paris"—was laid aside. But when they saw the grey hair of the sage, it was felt that the new Republic had appeared in character. Royalty murmured two formal sentences "with manly sincerity"; and the dazzled embassy withdrew. That night the Queen at cards desired Dr. Franklin to stand near by her, "and

70

as often as the game did not require her immediate attention, she took occasion to speak to him in very obliging terms." So reality came to Court in the early spring of 1778.

It came again to Versailles in the years that followed, seeking to pay the price of Dr. Franklin's treaty and M. de Vergennes' crusade. Once it walked in procession over wet pavements on a May morning in 1789, when the States General went down to their first meeting and Bishop Talleyrand limped in canonicals behind the bulk of M. de Mirabeau. Once again it streamed, under umbrellas, into a tennis court and took an oath. But it came for the last time on a dull October day, when Paris marched on Versailles and stood outside the palace and roared and waited. Somewhere beyond Meudon there was the crack of fowling-pieces in the woods, where the King was shooting. But the Queen was among the fading autumn flowers at Trianon. There was a pale gleam of sunshine; and she sat among the fallen leaves beside her grotto. Then a scared boy brought her a letter. She read, and turned for the last time towards the white house among the trees, where the leaves had fallen. She had a mind to run down the long walk to the Château. But she waited for the carriage; and they drove to the palace. The King returned from shooting; and as the light faded, the crowd still surged in the rain beyond the railings. That night they tried to sleep. La Fayette marched in at midnight and set his sentries. But Paris swept in at dawn. There was a little killing in the palace, as she ran half dressed through the great empty rooms to sanctuary with the King. Then, as the slow day came up, the place was cleared; and she stood with La Fayette on a great balcony above the *Cour de Marbre*. The square was packed with faces, and the busts in their niches looked down with blind marble eyes. The whole courtyard was thundering at her; someone pointed a musket; but La Fayette took her hand and knelt to her on the balcony. The clouds drifted above the palace; and after mid-day, as the rain shut down on the short autumn afternoon, they drove through the din down the long road to Paris. The guns, the pikes, the cries, the faces seemed to run all the way from the great square before the palace to the reeling city. For the King had left Versailles, left Trianon, left his woods and gardens and all the grace of gilt and candles. Before nightfall they were in the shadow of Paris. It screamed, thrust torches in their faces to look, and thundered round them like a sea in flood. But behind them at Versailles, in the silence and the darkness of the *Cour de Marbre*, the busts still looked down with their blind marble eyes.

IV

The coach jolted down the long street towards the packed and roaring square. He read his prayers in the closed carriage; and as the tall, shuttered houses slid past the window, he thought, he must have thought of a woman; of a tall girl with gleaming hair; of a smiling Queen among the trees at Trianon; of a haggard woman, who waited still in a tall tower with narrow windows. For he had loved her in his heavy, fumbling way; and as the coach jolted on, his love was ending. He drove down the long street between the silent houses, still reading in his corner; and the soldiers stood to watch the coach go by. They fingered their muskets or sat their horses in the cold morning; and the pale flame of burning matches flickered beside the guns, as the coach rumbled past. There was no other sound. The lonely carriage checked in the great square. But he read on in his corner; for the prayers in his hand were the prayers for the dying. When they were finished, he stepped out; and the day struck cold, as he stood for a moment at the foot of a ladder. An unceasing thunder of drums troubled his ears; and he said, a little sharply, "*Taisez-vous.*" Then he stripped his coat, and they bound him. He spoke a sentence; and as the drums broke out again, he looked out across the staring

73

faces towards the square palace and the palace garden and the pale winter sky. Perhaps he made as if to speak again. Perhaps he was silent to the end. He knew now, as he saw the tall machine, that he had lost her. If any cry rose in him, it was the formal, sweet lament which had wailed so often through the busy violins at Trianon. *J'ai perdu*—he was on the reeking planks now, above the crowd—*j'ai perdu mon Eurydice.* So she was lost; and he, at last, was silent; and still the violins come wailing down the wind in the last, unfinished melody of the French monarchy.

THE RIGHT HON. LORD NORTH, K. G.

> *Æquam   memento   rebus   in
> arduis
> Servare mentem.*
>
> HORACE.

THE RIGHT HON. LORD NORTH, K. G.

THERE is a sadness about statues. One commends it to those sensitive observers who distil their finer feelings from the aspect of old buildings, from bare trees seen against evening skies, from the slow, lunging flight of swans across still Irish lakes. They might do worse sometimes than spare attention for the depressing qualities of statues. Some, perhaps, are sadder than others. Statues in gardens have a neglected air, which makes an irresistible appeal. Memorial sculpture on consecrated ground has, possibly, an unfair advantage. But saddest of all are those strange effigies of public men with which all civilised communities love to punctuate their open spaces. They dispense a melancholy which challenges and baffles analysis. Perhaps it comes from the sad fact that their originals are almost always dead; for the statuary is never far removed from the monumental mason. Or it may derive from their appealing stillness in the midst of movement. They stand, those mournful watchers of the traffic, so motionless in their rigid draperies. Strangers disagree about their identity; birds alight upon them; shifting tides flow round their pedestals. But the hand is half raised in its eternal gesture; the blank eyes look down beneath the marble hair, through which no wind can blow; and the dismal effigy rides its spirited horse in a perpetual attitude of immobile triumph. One sometimes wonders that few passers stop to weep at the sad spectacle. For there is nothing frivolous about a statue: sculpture is, perhaps, the only art which has no humour.

But there is possibly a deeper reason for the sadness of statues. The sites for these depressing objects are selected with an exquisite perversity; and almost invariably they are erected in the wrong place. Statesmen at cross-roads may have a vague significance. But soldiers should not prance in palpably civilian streets; economists are out of place in gardens; and there is a positive discourtesy in placing royal persons just outside exclusive clubs. This ineptitude is not confined to the blunder which erects statues in the wrong quarter of the town. For quite often they are in the wrong country, too. Thus Lord Beaconsfield, whose main achievement was the preservation of the Turkish Empire, broods in bronze above the traffic in Parliament Square; whilst his effigy is almost unknown at Angora, and even in Constantinople that stately silhouette is

Lord North

From the drawing by Nathaniel Dance in the National Portrait Gallery (from a photograph by Emery Walker)

strangely unfamiliar. Columbus, by the same wild inconsequence, adorns a quay-side at Genoa, where a grateful Italy repays in bronze the debts of America; and Mr. Gladstone, whom thankful Greeks might have crowned with olive, confronts the indifferent Strand. A well-meaning committee, which ministers patiently to the exquisite misunderstanding of two continents, has even deepened the confusion by erecting in the ungrateful heart of London memorials to two benefactors of the United States. For one may venerate the work of Washington and Lincoln without desiring to see it so irrelevantly commemorated in the capital which one injured deeply and the other never affected in the least. The place of statues is dictated too often by the accident of birth, or the far stranger hazard of a subscription-list, too rarely by the truer test of a man's real achievement. His image, if we must have it, should stand where he leaves benefits behind him. The place for Napoleon is far less in France, which he helped to weaken, than in the grateful squares of Germany and Italy, which he united. That work should have earned him a throne in every *Sieges-allee*, a marble niche in every Valhalla ever hewn from the colossal quarry of German gratitude. King George III is out of place in Cockspur Street. That neat military figure, when America pays her historical debts, will ride down

Broadway. For he helped more than most men for whom the claim is made to found the United States. A similar piety should impel every town in the Union to erect a statue of Lord North. With that monument in view, these notes may serve, perhaps, as a foundation for the public appeal. A modest pedestal might proclaim that, though not strictly a Son of Liberty, he was yet a father of the Revolution.

This embarrassed man, who was (with his sovereign and General Washington) the official architect of the Republic, was a person of family. He had an ancestor whom rare political agility enabled successively to support Lady Jane Grey, take office from Queen Mary, and twice entertain Elizabeth. Another fought at Blenheim and had a sister—the marvel of her age—who "emaciated herself with study" and, becoming by these drastic means familiar with the Latin, Greek, and Oriental tongues, died of a sedentary distemper. As King Charles followed King James and King James succeeded to King Charles, Norths married judiciously and throve at Court; whilst younger sons embraced the Church, the law, and even letters. A pious North preached before Charles II at Newmarket, and raised (it is to be hoped) his hearer's thoughts from that low environment. Another, fortified by his precept that a

glass of wine is the equivalent of exercise for sedentary persons, even scaled the Woolsack and, sedentary
there, kept his sovereign's conscience. That aphor-
ism was perhaps the family's chief contribution to
medicine, just as its highest achievement in physical
science was the discovery of the springs at Tun-
bridge Wells.

This little nest of pensioners twittered happily
through the first sunny years of the Eighteenth
Century. The reigning North took the head of the
long dining-table at Wroxton; and attendant Norths
admired the pictures (the Lord Keeper was extremely
fine, and there was a lively portrait of Prince Henry
"about twelve years old, drawing his sword to kill
a stag") or enjoyed the noble prospect of a lake,
which tumbled obligingly, with due regard to the
laws of perspective, over "a fine cascade." The
seventh Baron served his country in the Bedchamber
of Frederick, Prince of Wales. He added a library
to Wroxton, built a new chapel "in a pretty Gothic
taste," and erected an obelisk in the park to his royal
master *in loci amoenitatem et memoriam adventûs
ejus.* Such loyalty was hardly too well rewarded
when the Prince stood godfather to his companion's
heir, and the happy child received the name of
Frederick. Thus early was the young brow of North
fanned by the breeze of royal favour. His father was

assiduous as Lord of the Bedchamber to the Prince of Wales, rose to be Governor to his royal son, and dreamed of an earldom. The accomplished Baron (had he not built a library?) directed the studies of Prince George; and by a queer conjunction the father of Lord North played tutor for five months to George III. But the dreadful tennis-ball removed his master; he died in French and, with a corresponding elegance, there were cards in the next room. As the busy candles moved about Carlton House, his Lord of the Bedchamber was sent through the spring night to take the news along the Mall. There were cards at the palace, too, that evening; and the sovereign, who was looking over a table, received the sad announcement with mild surprise. So the little Prince became a Prince of Wales; and his noble Governor was superseded by an Earl, although Mr. Walpole thought that "there was no objection but his having a glimpse of parts more than the new one." But he got his earldom.

So the latest North breathed an exalted air, whilst his father was away at Kew in waiting; and the little Frederick bore the proud burden of his royal name through the big rooms at Wroxton. There was a strange look of his Hanoverian godfather in the vague, protruding eyes; and as he aged, he even seemed to carry loyalty to the odd length of reproducing his

sovereign's profile. An arch whisper gave him credit
for royal blood. But there was no ground for the
scandal beyond the faint, surviving flavour of Prince
Frederick's reputation. His little godson was, indeed,
to serve the royal House, which he so resembled.
But the boy was not yet in the King's service. His
mother died; and his father, a frequent bridegroom,
married two more for him. A small step-brother
shared his chicken-pox; and the young mind was
sent to Eton, to be formed for seven years upon that
anvil of true sagacity, Latin verse. A candid tutor
called him "a blundering blockhead, and if you are
Prime Minister, it will always be the same"; whilst
more graceful pens commended his blushing parents
upon his judgment, taste, and scholarship, adding
(more credibly, perhaps) that he was extremely
popular. From these scholastic triumphs, and the
performance of a small part in Addison's *Cato* before
the Prince of Wales, he passed to Oxford, still whispering from her towers (so Gothic, yet so refined)
the last enchantments of the Middle Age. An ornament of Trinity College, he was rewarded almost at
once with a Master's degree in recognition, no doubt,
of his noble birth and of that "uniform attention to
the minuter points of duty" which so impressed his
tutor. The course of his studies is unknown; but
there, or in private reading, he acquired that graceful

familiarity with stray fragments of dead languages which marked him for public life. The boy was capable and witty; although upon one occasion he wrote, with rare ineptitude, to congratulate his father on having the gout. This ill-timed felicitation earned a stern denial that gout was "a matter for congratulation when it comes to a healthy person, though it may be a great relief to a person labouring under worse distempers," together with the more suitable reflection of his suffering parent that "the Christian religion . . . seems to be the only solid foundation for constant cheerfulness."

But Latin tags and Court connexions were not his sole equipment. He trod, with rare persistence, the long road of the Grand Tour, posting industriously about Europe in pursuit of learning. He visited Leyden in search of the Law of Nations; he lay at Leipzig and was distressed by a "want of good butter"; he found an Italian master at Vienna and a ball at Milan; parties in Rome were more frequent than in Mr. Walpole's day, when that traveller had disconsolately watched the nobility "mope in a vast palace with two miserable tapers, and two or three monsignori"; and there was still, there was always Paris. But he brought home with him something more than the usual catalogue of inns and post-chaises. His French was fluent; he danced "the most graceful

minuet of any young man of his day"; he could be
agreeable in Italian; and he possessed the rarer
accomplishment of German recitation, including
within his range an invocation which began *Komm,
Doris, komm.* So this cheerful young man, whose
ton was perfect in spite of a poor appearance, came
upon the town. He had a turn of wit, a fund of
classical quotation, and a father. The choice of a
career was plain; and at twenty-two he entered
Parliament.

His rise was discreetly slow. At twenty-five he
seconded the Address; at twenty-seven he got a
place. He roared with agreeable impartiality for
Mr. Pitt, Lord Bute, and Mr. Grenville. He vin-
dicated the cause of order against the atrocious
Wilkes. He raised what Mr. Walpole termed his
bellow in defence of ministers; and for political principles this vociferous understrapper, whose thick
voice "rumbled" like stage thunder at the Whigs,
seemed to share the strange ideal of Mr. Pitt and
his sovereign. For both men (and with them Lord
North) believed that England should be governed
by national ministers, uncontrolled by faction. That
belief, which was challenged by the stricter Whigs,
united the queer trio. It lit in Mr. Pitt an unwavering faith in the non-party dictatorship of Mr. Pitt;
it sent the King groping vaguely after Bolingbroke's

ideal of a *Patriot King*, who should "espouse no party"; and it kept Lord North in command of an odd crew of King's Friends at the national helm, where (like the incautious Palinurus) he not infrequently slept. Thus the same road, which had led to Minden and Plassey and the Heights of Abraham, ended at Yorktown and Saratoga; for North was, in many ways, the heir of Chatham. Indeed, this queer political paternity was almost acknowledged, when he urged an angry King in later years to increase Pitt's pension. The sage disciple kept his place, whilst the King conducted his first experiment in national government. But when the Whigs returned in force and the blameless Rockingham made him an offer, he "goggled his eyes, and groped in his money-pocket; more than half consented; nay, so much more that when he got home he wrote an excuse to Lord Rockingham"; and so preserved the chastity of his ideal.

The Whigs were tried and found even themselves wanting. Faction had failed; and Chatham marched back to place behind the national banner. Remembering North's patriotic ideals, he offered him a minor office in a letter of tremendous courtesy. The efficiency of the King's service, the life of his government, and the continued happiness of Chatham appeared to depend upon Lord North's acceptance of the post of Joint Paymaster-General. He complied; and the world went on again. But the stout young man had higher prospects. His gifts were scarcely meretricious; but the House of Commons forms strange attachments, and he was undeniably liked by that queer assembly. Twelve years in Parliament had made him a sound debater. His manner, as Burke observed it—"the noble lord who spoke last, after extending his right leg a full yard before his left, rolling his flaming eyes and moving his ponderous frame, has at length opened his mouth" —was deplorable. But an easy wit and his unfailing temper saved him. The solemn Grenville talked gravely of his "great promise and high qualifications"; and even Townshend could cheerfully point out "that great, heavy, booby-looking seeming changeling" and prophesy with rare precision that "if anything should happen to me, he will succeed to my place, and very shortly after come to be First Commissioner of the Treasury." Brilliant as ever, Townshend fulfilled his own prediction, died, and left the Treasury to North, who was promoted Chancellor of the Exchequer at thirty-five. Three years of apprenticeship remained, in which he displayed once more his "uniform attention to the minuter points of duty," introduced judicious Budgets, and earned a reputation for sober qualities. But the King was growing restive as ministers became more Whiggish; and at last, on January 23, 1770, at "40 minutes past 10 a.m.," he turned to North, and North accepted.

They were an odd pair, the two young men with their smooth faces and protruding eyes. Friendship and official duty had united their fathers; but the sons, with a rarer unanimity, seemed to share a single profile. Both brows, both chins receded with a common design; and below the powdered regularity of dressed hair each pair of eyes stared hard in the comic fierceness of weak sight. The King was thirty-two, and knew his mind. The minister was thirty-eight and, more judicious, knew his place. For, inclined to compliance by his natural good manners, North held a doctrine, which rendered his sovereign almost irresistible. Sharing Lord Chatham's queer *marotte* that party was less than country, he added a yet stranger notion of his own that the country was personified in its King. For him the voice that spoke in jerks was England's; an embodied nation showered minute instructions upon him; and when his country issued its orders from the Queen's House at "2 min. pt. 5 p.m." and "57 min. pt. 11 a.m.," disobedience was almost treasonable. Such a minister was unlikely to defy the Crown. Indeed, since he firmly denied the existence of his own office, it was doubtful how far he was prepared to dominate his colleagues. For his daughter remembered how "he would never allow us to call him Prime Minister," saying, "there was no such thing in the British Constitution"; and he once told the House of Commons that "he did not think the constitution authorised such a character. He stood responsible as one of His Majesty's Cabinet Council, but not as that animal called a Prime Minister." Some vague duties of leadership were performed by a functionary termed "Minister of the House of Commons." But Dr. Johnson, ever avid of authority, could complain that "there is now no Prime Minister; he is only agent for Government in the House of Commons." Cabinets were intermittent; ministers rarely shared responsibility for the acts of their colleagues; and the King was steadily becoming head of his own Executive. So, in his duties as well as in himself, the new minister was hardly such stuff as Pitts are made of.

This obliging person, who managed the House of Commons with his monocle and his little jokes, brought in a reputation for "very good parts, quickness, great knowledge, and" (strangest praise of all) "activity." His virtues and, to a large extent, his work were those of a party Whip. He smiled; he promised places; he sometimes threatened; but he offended no one. Argument was mainly left to his Law Officers, to the terrifying play of Thurlow's eyebrows, and the painfully precise articulation of Wedderburn, still striving to repress an irrepressible Scot accent. But majorities obeyed the bland, persuasive man, who sat between them and seemed to sleep as dreamlessly as though the Treasury Bench had been a Chinese summer-house at Wroxton. Mr. Gibbon might quote Virgil upon the fate of Palinurus; writers of catches were mildly disrespectful about *Boreas;* and caricaturists revelled in the cosy outline of "the Badger," who (with the Fox) was their delight for a generation. But North's tellers always brought back a majority from the lobby. Political management was his art; and for four years his sovereign rarely corresponded with him upon larger topics. The ministry was engaged upon a solution of the problem of Indian government, which displayed a real sense of responsibility for Indian welfare. Its Canada policy, with toleration for French law and Catholic worship, startled the neighbouring Protestants of Philadelphia into illiberal protests against its bold treatment of "a religion that has deluged your island in blood, and dispersed impiety, bigotry, persecution, murder, and rebellion through every part of the world." But the King's frequent minutes to his minister dealt with the more immediate problems of division-lists, incumbencies, Court vacancies, and Regius Professorships; until, at "46 min. pt. 6 p.m." on a winter evening in 1774, he discussed "the mode of compelling Boston to submit to whatever may be thought necessary." General Gage had been at the palace using heroic language about "lyons" and "lambs"; and his delighted sovereign, flown with these lively metaphors, presented Lord North with the American question.

The prospect was uninviting. Other problems might be solved by an application of common sense. North and his colleagues had shown a real capacity for imperial matters; the India Act and the Canadian settlement were just and intelligent. For in both cases they had been free to determine policy without regard to past errors or old commitments. But America, in 1774, had a long and awkward history. Almost every group in English politics was committed by some former action to opposing the Colonial claims. Mr. Grenville had taxed; the Whigs had repealed the tax but, with unhappy pedantry, reserved the right; Mr. Townshend had taxed again. North himself at the Exchequer maintained the tea duty; and as Prime Minister he "heartily wished to repeal the whole of the law, from this conciliating principle, if there had been a possibility of repealing it without giving up that just right which I shall ever wish the mother country to possess, the right of taxing the Americans." That dismal point of law, upon which he conceived "the controlling supremacy of England" to rest, was common ground in almost every quarter of the House. Whigs, King's Friends, and Tories were equally committed to it. No Ajax could have˜defied that collective lightning. Even Lord Chatham, by the intermittent glareˈof his suburban Sinai, had desired somehow to assert "the sovereign authority of this country over the colonies"; and Mr. Burke still praised the fatal pedantry of the Declaratory Act.

Boston was out against taxation; and North's problem in 1774 was to determine the direction of British policy. But he was hardly free to choose. For his main concern was to keep a majority for the King's government; and if he wavered upon taxation, he could not take ten members with him into the lobby. That factor was decisive. Nine years of tangled politics had created a permanent majority for American taxation; and North, whatever his opinions, could not defy it. The King, the Whigs, the Tories all dictated his decision; and, upon grounds within the comprehension of any party Whip, he settled the future of the Colonial Empire. So, with a failing heart, he resolved to break the will of Boston. Another factor must, one feels, have inclined him to the same inevitable choice. The

Colonial cause had unfortunately become the cause of disorder. It mobbed; it tarred; it feathered; it fired revenue cutters and boarded East-Indiamen at anchor. England had lived, was living through an awkward phase of popular tumult, in which the sinister grimace of Mr. Wilkes seemed to preside over a whirling Brocken of Middlesex electors. The sawyers rose; the sailors marched on Westminster; the coal-heavers "robbed in companies, and murdered wherever they came." Gin and torchlight flared together in the London streets; and a cool observer of the English scene in 1774 must have predicted that the mob would fire the Tower of London long before their friends in Paris ventured to storm the Bastille. In this uneasy stir ministers were unnaturally firm. North, always steady, watched a mob break up his carriage, heard the crash of glass when the stones came through his windows, and saw his postilion reel in the saddle, as a pistol shot cracked on Hounslow Heath. But the stubborn mood in which they rode out the storm was unfriendly to quiet negotiation with popular risings. Seen from three thousand miles away, Boston was not unlike the London mob. So, both in London and overseas, North and the King held firm. They turned on Boston as they had turned on Southwark; and Boston made the war.

From that point the slope dropped steeply away. In '74, when the Revolution seemed an affair of street-fighting in a single town, and the Boston Port Act was to save the Empire, he still hoped that "four or five frigates will do the business without any military force." In '75 he was for non-taxation, "ready to punish, but . . . nevertheless, ready to forgive"; insisting only that the Americans should tax themselves, and scandalising strict patriots by his disgraceful willingness to "treat with rebels." But the repression of Boston had done its work. The shots at Lexington deepened, after eight weeks, into a steady roll of musketry on Bunker's Hill; and North had unintentionally made the United States.

His conduct of the war lacked fire. His sovereign might exclaim that "blows must decide," and cheerfully announce that "every means of distressing America must meet with my concurrence." The royal pen was full of plans, and angry Admirals gathered in every corner of the House of Commons. But the Prime Minister had little taste for strategy. With an intelligence rare among civilian statesmen in time of war, he left the war to soldiers. His distaste was deepened by a vague foreboding of the result. Whilst the official imagination of 1777 watched Burgoyne and Clinton racing for laurels along the Hudson, North could write that a despatch

94

"is very unpleasant and begins to make me feel rather uncomfortable"; and even before the news of Saratoga, he was half inclined to "take advantage of the flourishing state of our affairs to get out of this d——d war." The flavour of defeat depressed him; his health was poor; he broke his arm in a riding accident; and money worries (since he was an honest steward of the public corruption) weighed on him. After Saratoga the French, with ostentatious chivalry, joined the winning side; the fleet was unready; the armies fumbled vaguely about New England; and North, in a final effort for peace, seemed to acknowledge independence "not *verbally* yet *virtually*." He turned, as men in danger always turned, to Chatham. But the King, who had a steadier nerve and detested unruly genius, clung with embarrassing affection to Lord North; and Chatham sat muttering at Hayes until the day when, led in by two young men, he limped on crutches to his place, made his last strangled speech, and fell gasping in the House of Lords.

The war dragged on; and North interminably tried to escape from office. But his inexorable correspondent at the Queen's House pointed to duty, appealed to friendship, alluded to desertion in the hour of danger, referred with touching frequency to the Constitution—"the most beautiful combination that ever was framed"—and even, with rarer condescension, to the feelings of a man. "Year after year," as North said later, "I entreated to be allowed to resign, but I was not allowed." He played like an actor who dislikes his part. "I hate," he wrote, "my situation." Indeed, the emotion was not surprising. Most men would have been broken by those years. Revolution in America, war with France, Spain, and Holland, a growing menace in Ireland, and a new war in India composed the picture. The soldiers failed; even the sailors were only intermittently successful. There was an alarming interlude, when for four days the town was mad for "No Popery" and Lord George Gordon. The sky was red over London with the dull glare of burning houses, and strange figures crouched and ran with blue cockades and broken railings carried at the trail like pikes. As the prospect darkened, even Parliament found its voice; and North's majorities began to dwindle. British defeats are the most sustaining nourishment of British Oppositions; and the Whig murmur deepened in the gathering gloom. The pack was after him. It charged "the noble Lord in the blue ribbon" with incompetence, treachery, stupidity, even (on a day when he had lost a son) with corruption. But he struggled on, until the news of Yorktown came; and North took it "as he would have taken a ball in his breast, opening his arms and exclaiming wildly, 'O God! it is all over.' " Four months later he was out and subsided with a smile into private life, whilst Dr. Johnson grimly entered in his little book: "The Ministry is dissolved; I prayed with Francis and gave thanks." The Colonies were free; and North had earned his statue.

He had a second phase. But it need hardly figure on his American pedestal, since it relates to purely domestic politics. He inclined, like so many statesmen who have emerged from wars, to Coalition. Perhaps this odd taste, which is rarely shared for long by their countrymen, was strengthened in him by his unfailing geniality. Lacking in bitterness, North was "irreconcilable to no man"; greeting invective with a short-sighted smile; poking sly fun at angry gentlemen on the opposite benches; calling to Fox after a savage attack on ministers, "Charles, I am glad you did not fall on me to-day, for you were in full feather." His Pittite training had made him more sensitive to national than to party interests; and perhaps his experience as manager of the King's majority had left him a trifle sceptical as to the precise doctrinal distinction between Whig and Tory. This agreeable temper took him into the Coalition; and startled voters, who had thrilled responsive to the catalogue of his crimes enunciated by the indignant Fox, observed the strange union of the accuser and the accused, whilst inelegant ballad-mongers chanted the nuptials of the Fox and the Badger. Even while it lasted, the scene was scarcely credible. The political public always insists upon a certain reality in its disputes; and North's fatal lack of asperity, that easiest of all political virtues, was a grave handicap. Public faith was equally shaken by the echoes of defeat, which still hung about his name. Men could hardly forget that

> Lord North, for twelve years with his war and contracts,
> The people he nearly had laid on their backs.

So the Coalition, inspired perhaps by a confused recollection of one Pitt, collapsed before another; and North passed out of history. He lasted for eight years longer, making little jokes among his children at Bushey, enduring that intolerable groom "that puts papa in a passion," hearing (for he was quite blind now) his daughter reading Shakespeare. Then he died in that wild August of 1792, which brought in a new world. For North, who had helped to make one, was spared another.

THE RIGHT HON. EARL OF CHATHAM

> *One minded like the weather,*
> *most unquietly.*
> KING LEAR.

THE RIGHT HON. EARL OF CHATHAM

THERE is a charm in endings. Slightly, perhaps, in poetry, but more acutely in public speeches and the longer forms of musical composition one becomes aware of it. The dying fall, the *envoi*, the peroration strike upon grateful ears; athletes become almost interesting in their last lap; curtains, which rose in silence, fall to applause. For it is always an ending, rarely a beginning, that we welcome. The start of a horse-race is a tepid spectacle; but the finish stirs multitudes. Playgoers, indifferent to the opening moves, demand a happy ending. And who (with deference to Motley) would open *The Rise of the Dutch Republic* when he could read *The Decline and Fall of the Roman Empire?* The taste for endings is a human instinct. All the world will watch a sunset, while sunrises are abandoned to the insincere appreciation of a limited and self-conscious sect. Gray, with consummate art, began his *Elegy* with an ending; and the last words of statesmen are more eagerly awaited than their finest speeches.

A great man, one feels, is never greater than when

he is no longer present. His origins are dull; his career is blameless. But greatness seems to grow upon him as the shadows lengthen. The night draws on; and when a still figure faces a sinking sun, it takes on the dignity of an ending. Such phases have a rare charm. Napoleon on the island, his tired nephew among the trees at Chislehurst, the long decline of Gladstone draw the fancy by their vague outlines. Perhaps they lingered too long and died too late. But is there half the charm in Wolfe and Nelson, in Robespierre and Danton, who died in time and never aged? That is why one wonders that Lord Rosebery, who has felt the fascination of Napoleon's last phase and spent a lifetime in his own, left Chatham's undescribed.

It was the oddest epilogue. The young hero, who startled the world into admiration in Sir Robert Walpole's time by a free use of the epithets "execrable" and "flagitious"; the Rupert (if one may transfer the compliment) of debate, who was "the meteor" of the House of Commons, who stung—in the alarmed hearing of young Mr. Walpole—"like an angry wasp" and, mixing comedy with his "Gorgon's head," towered into ridicule, which "lasts and rises, flash after flash, for an hour and a half," and left his dazzled hearer gathering up "the glittering

Lord Chatham, 1777

From the picture by R. Brompton in the National Portrait Gallery (from a photograph
by Emery Walker)

splinters"; the minister who for five incomparable years persuaded his countrymen to share his strange confidence "that I can save this country and that nobody else can," and rewarded them with the steady boom of the Park guns, announcing victory; the conqueror, who won America in Germany and India in both; the unchallenged master of his country, who kept the Bath crowd standing whilst he sipped his water in the Pump Room, and had become (with the Tower, Blenheim Palace, Stowe, and the Quakers) an object of interest to enquiring foreigners; this amazing constellation of success was curiously dimmed by failure in its later phases.

That figure never lost its strange attraction; the nose was masterful to the end; and the piercing eye—that eye which, in Shelburne's phrase, "would cut a diamond"—alarmed his latest hearers. But as he withdrew into the equivocal half-light of his closing years, his unrivalled armoury seemed somehow to become ineffectual. Within ten years of his salvo of victories little Mr. Walpole could write disrespectful things about "an old beauty in an unfashionable dress" and "old Myra in her fardingale." Such irreverence would have been unthinkable in 1760, whilst the lightnings played about the mountain from which he issued his commandments. But ten years later the same lightning was, somehow, a less alarming spectacle. He still flashed and thundered. But perhaps the rocks were riven a shade less frequently. The awful mountain itself was sometimes invisible in drifting clouds; and there was a growing feeling that the storm was muttering at a safer distance. For by his triumphant conduct of the Seven Years' War he had taken his place in history; and it is rarely easy for an historical character to play a lively part in current politics. That deprivation was, in a sense, the price which he paid for his transcendent glory. He had chosen to rival successfully the achievements of the Elizabethans; and in doing so, he had attained something of their remoteness. He had scaled his pedestal; and eager contemporaries hardly looked to statues for advice.

Yet as his energies declined, he resisted the immobile dignity of marble; and for fifteen years his country was afforded the strange spectacle of an effigy from Westminster Abbey in active politics. It was a queer, sometimes a terrifying vision. Perhaps he had always been a little like the statue of the Commander. His epistolary style, indeed, was never anything but marmoreal. But in his later manner the resemblance positively grew upon him, as he moved stiffly to his place, glared around, and launched upon a hollow speech. The alarming episode continued until his last mutter died away in the

House of Lords. The unnerving figure, with its tormented eyes almost invisible below the peak of a great wig, was so indisputably a *revenant*, that few observers would have started if it had clanked a ghostly chain. For there is about all his later speeches an oddly posthumous quality. They seem like half-remembered quotations from himself; there is almost an air of *pastiche* about them. Even to himself, one feels, he must have seemed unreal. Indeed there was in his last phase a conscious effort to depict an Elder Statesman. He almost ceased to be a man and became a magnificent impersonation. The nods, the piercing stares, the careful lighting, the oracular utterance seem to come rather from the baroque imagination of a romantic actor than from the instincts of an elderly English gentleman in poor health. He was posed; he was draped; he was lit; he was almost set to music. In those accomplished hands the crutch and flannels of his infirmity became incomparable "properties," as the huddled figure sat mumbling his mysterious lines. What a part it would have been for Sir Henry Irving, if Lord Chatham had not played it.

This strange decline began early. Even in his great days, when the victory guns were still smoking in the Park, he was almost intolerably odd. The

Pitts were unpleasantly remarkable for their oddity. The family abounded in strange, explosive sisters; and an elder brother was muttering somewhere abroad over an interminable grievance. So it was not surprising that the King's minister comported himself like the Mogul; and every spring his country's business waited upon his annual illness. But the nation, never quick to detect eccentricity in high places, seemed to notice nothing, although already a squib was faintly irreverent about *Gulielmo Bombasto de Podagra*, and politicians were inclined to be a trifle sceptical when at awkward moments he "gave himself a terrible fit of the gout"; some-one, indeed, was even found to doubt whether it was "a real or political fit." But the mass of his countrymen, to whom a symptom always connotes a fund of inexhaustible enjoyment, appeared to find the impressive mechanism of his ailments almost endearing; since an embittered satirist could complain that

> The very *doorkeepers it touches*
> To see him tottering on *crutches*.
>
> .   .   .   .   .   .
>
> The groundlings cry alas! poor man!
> How ill he is! how pale! how wan!

That was a very British cry; and it may be wondered that no other statesman has so triumphantly exploited the national taste for pathology. Even in time of peace, one feels, a reasonably ailing minister must be in an exceptionally strong position. But in war-time, with laurels showering in three continents like leaves in an autumn gale, the valetudinarian was quite impregnable. His crutch became a standard, his flannels a banner; and his pervading oddity passed muster for the trifling mannerism of a national champion. For nations are strangely uncritical of successful war-ministers.

But with peace the world became more critical. There was, as yet, no visible decline of his powers. The flow of thought was unimpeded; the head, when necessary, was erect. The voice was still full, as when:

> He woo'd the fair with manly sense,
>   And, flattery apart,
> By dint of sterling eloquence
>   Subdued Corinna's heart.

But, lacking his favourite "thorough-bass of drums and trumpets," it began to seem a shade less resonant. Perhaps the gaunt figure had been more telling against the familiar background of war. Seen on a peaceful stage, it had something of the futility of a gentleman portrayed in a martial attitude before a velvet curtain; the stern eye, the hand upon the sword-hilt in the foreground seem to demand a charge of cavalry, some drifting smoke, or a few floating spars in the middle distance. Without them, Pitt was a little lost in the first years after the peace. Even his admirers hardly knew what to applaud; and soon an irreverent caricaturist could depict a swathed, majestic foot emerging from an inn door at the sign of "Popularity the blown bladder by W. P." During the war, indeed, popularity had been strained a little by his pension and his wife's peerage. There was a tendency to deplore this solicitude for "a paltry annuity, a long-necked peeress, and a couple of Grenvilles"; and the alarming tribune was never a conciliatory figure. But victory was a rare substitute for popular graces; and so long as the guns were firing, Pitt continued surprisingly to woo the affections of his countrymen with a manner that appeared to have been borrowed from Marius in the ruins of Carthage.

But with the peace he became merely enigmatic. The London mob, having no further victories to cheer, turned to the equally congenial exercise of hooting ministers. Its exclamation was, on the whole, correct; since the King's servants were inefficient and not particularly constitutional. But as mobs almost invariably reach the right conclusions for the wrong reasons, it hooted upon the oddest grounds. Believing Bute to be a Scotsman (which

he was) and the King's mother to be immoral
(which she was not), it roared against Prerogative;
and for these singular reasons George's dismal experiment in personal government became unpopular. It
deserved, indeed, to become so on more rational
grounds. For England in 1763 had outlived the
need for autocracy. There was a growing habitua-
tion to the forms, at least, of self-government; and
the Eighteenth Century was no place for Tudors.
This odd experiment in monarchy provoked a popular reaction, and the City became a slightly unexpected home of English liberties. Deep-voiced aldermen harangued their liveries on Magna Carta, and
the Guildhall echoed with the indignant eloquence
of Common Councillors. The City had always been
the stronghold of Pitt's popularity, and resistance to
an encroaching monarchy might well have provided
suitable exercise for a Great Commoner out of
employment. But the strange man made no movement. The crowd was left without an adequate
leader; and mobs, which wished to cheer for liberty,
were forced by Pitt's default to shout for Wilkes.

He was, indeed, curiously disabled from heading
the opposition to the King; since he shared his strange
heresy. Both men, for different reasons, disbelieved
in party. Pitt's vision was of a nation united behind
its minister; the King's, behind its king. In either

dream the restless figures of British politics were to be conducted to a non-party Nirvana of beatific immobility, a static condition in which Pitt (or the King) should preside eternally over an unprotesting state. So both were equally averse from "faction," as opposition is invariably termed by persons to whom it is distasteful. Non-party men are rarely believers in active opposition, since they intend to be perpetually in office; and Pitt had once prescribed that "true political moderation consists in not opposing the measures of Government except when great and national objects are at stake: to oppose upon any other foot is certainly faction." It was his firm belief that "every man ought to show himself for the whole . . . Be one people!" So he was disinclined to systematic opposition and not unduly shocked by George's attempt to substitute the Crown for party. A further cause, perhaps, kept him immobile. The King's return to Tudor habits might scandalise his contemporaries; but it need hardly scare a statesman who was so manifestly an Elizabethan minister astray in the Eighteenth Century. For Pitt, one feels, must have been more at home with Burleigh than with Mr. Burke. He faced the French in the defiant temper which had once confronted Spain; he sent his sailors round the world upon errands which would have been congenial to Drake; and it need hardly shock him, if there was a touch of Tudor in his King. Indeed, he saw the mysterious glory of the Crown too plainly to appreciate the fine shades of the Whig doctrinaires. His irritable sovereign might call him "a trumpet of sedition"; but after the first wild oats of his early opposition he seemed to become a monarchist of almost religious intensity, leaving office at the King's pleasure, accepting it only upon his willing invitation, and parading a tremendous deference to royalty in the Closet, where scared courtiers watched the slow descent of that imperial nose to meet those ailing knees. The King stirred in him some of those sentiments, which were later inspired in Mr. Burke by the more impressive spectacle of Windsor Castle. It was a romantic fascination that is fairly comparable with Mr. Disraeli's. He saw the embodiment of his country in a stout young man with prominent eyes; and, seeing it, the old mystic was rarely capable of marked dissent.

So the eager mob was defrauded of its natural leader by Pitt's strange convictions. For such sentiment and such genuflexions were scarcely compatible with brisk opposition to the Crown; and his voice was barely audible above the growing tumult of the years in which Mr. Wilkes made democracy disreputable. Successful demagogues are rarely unac-

111

countable; and that, to an impatient observer, was precisely the quality of Pitt's keen, but tangential, mind. Even Shelburne noticed how greatly he "depended on taking quick turns, which was his forte." Crowds love to follow; but they rarely follow an elusive scent. They prefer their leaders labelled in plain figures; and no label was secure for long on Pitt. First visible to his countrymen in spirited opposition to the Crown, he had recurred in respectful service to it. Crossing the stage with a lively denunciation of European wars, he had re-entered hastily from the opposite side and directed, without a change of make-up, the most successful campaigns since Marlborough. He seemed to disdain the practice of consistency, that easy virtue, which provides dull politicians with a convenient substitute for judgment. Perhaps he scarcely needed it himself: one does not ask a Major Prophet to be consistent. But a touch of this common quality would have been so helpful to his supporters. For it is unfortunately true that in politics consistent mediocrities are simpler to follow than Major Prophets. Pitt had, indeed, his steady vision of public service. It burned bright above the roaring streets and the flushed faces in the House of Commons; it gleamed uncertainly through the trees at Hayes; and he followed it like a star. But the crowd, seeing only the strange windings of his political course, watched him a little sadly and began to doubt.

It was, indeed, bewildering to observe the Great Commoner living amiably under the King's experiment in autocracy. He was rude, in his stately fashion, to Mr. Grenville. He boomed vaguely about the liberty of the subject and the impropriety of general warrants (of which he had issued three). But he roared them so gently that three times in the two years which followed the peace he was invited by his sovereign to form a ministry. That, one feels, is the surest evidence that Pitt was harmless. His harmlessness, indeed, increased with failing health. His gout became a ruling passion; Bath was the centre of his universe, where he could "crawl to the pump" and sip his water; and soon he was known, as Mr. Walpole said, "only by tradition." Out of doors the world of men moved up and down with cheers for Wilkes and groans for Bute. But Pitt was fading silently into the half-light of sick-rooms. Sometimes the hand, sometimes the foot gave trouble; forks and pens became awkward implements; and at intervals he felt strange cravings to be left alone in silence.

But as he failed, there was one topic that seemed to engage his wandering attention. Mr. Grenville, harassed for revenue, had taxed America; and Pitt, who had saved, had even in part created the empire, held strange opinions on the subject. They drummed in his head, as he lay in his bed at Burton Pynsent or stared gloomily at the elegant regularity of the Bath crescents. His opinions, his empire, his colonists haunted the sick man's mind through the summer weeks, when those lively taxpayers were burning stamped paper in Boston at one shilling the sheet folio. But his strength revived at the turn of the year; and in the first days of 1766 he came to town to "deliver his mind and heart on the state of America." That topic engaged him for the remainder of his life; it was the theme of the last movement, a strong thread of melody which ran through the strange discords of twelve jangled years. He was old; he was ill; he was not (the fault was his own) attached to any party. The gaunt figure seemed to start on a lonely adventure by a failing light. Almost, since he had always seemed an odd survival from an earlier time, he might have worn armour; a lance would hardly have been surprising in that hand. He rode (for Pitt was always spiritually on horseback) alone and slowly; and as the challenge of that angular figure came up against the sky, his nickname had never fitted "Don William Quixote" more wickedly well.

So, with distressed America for his Dulcinea and

grotesquely squired by one of his aldermen, Pitt set out on his last ride. He never finished the adventure. The opinions of this amazing champion were oddly compounded. He believed "that the Parliament has a right to bind, to restrain America." He maintained that "we may bind their trade, confine their manufactures." But he insisted "that this Kingdom has no right to lay a tax upon the colonies." A more logical mind might, perhaps, have found some difficulty in reconciling this faith in the fiscal freedom of the Americans with his fierce insistence upon "the power of Parliament . . . known in the colonies by the prohibition of their carrying a hat to market over the line of one province into another, or by breaking down a loom in the most distant corner of the British empire in America; and if this power were denied, I would not permit them to manufacture a lock of wool or a horseshoe or a hobnail." For his resistance to American taxation was founded upon a doctrine of British sovereignty, which in General Gage would be regarded as an outrage upon liberty. But it was Pitt's merit that he was never logical. British institutions rarely yield their secret to logical minds; and in his greatest utterance he rose superior to all reason and proclaimed a triumphant faith in the co-existence of an irresistible force and an immovable post. So when he followed his insistence upon

115

sovereignty with a hoarse ejaculation that "I rejoice that America had resisted," and by way of practical advice quoted, in a gentler voice,

> Be to her faults a little blind,
> Be to her virtues very kind,

this glorious blend of two incompatible doctrines with a policy inconsistent with either was more than logical; for it was right.

His cryptic message was delivered within the limits of a single debate; and a bewildered ministry of his disciples endeavoured to execute it. The Stamp Act was repealed; but since the Whig intelligence was unequal to the subtlety of his conviction that a sovereign Parliament with absolute authority to prohibit manufacture could not impose a tax, the repeal was accompanied by a reassertion "that Great Britain hath and ought to have full right and power to bind the Americans in all cases whatsoever." He blessed the repeal, insisted once again upon his curious distinction, and left for Bath; whilst grateful Americans drank toasts, preached sermons, and voted statues in his honour. There was a gratifying tumult in the streets, although the cheers had perhaps more reference to his past victories than to his present opinions; and ministers showed an almost pathetic anxiety to carry out the lightest, most enigmatic wish of the alarming hierophant, who was to call them with amused contempt "the gentle warblers of the grove."

But before he went he expressed, with an odd revulsion to his old ideals of government, a singular "wish, for the sake of our dear country, that all our factions might cease. I could wish that a ministry might be fixed, such as the King could appoint and the public approve; that in it men might be properly adapted to the employments they are appointed to, and whose names are known in Europe, to convey an idea of dignity to this Government both at home and abroad. If ever I were again admitted, as I have been, into the Royal presence, it would be independent of any personal connection whatsoever." This seemed ungrateful to the Whigs; but the King, detecting the non-party note, discerned in Pitt the natural successor of Lord Bute and Mr. Grenville. Pitt might be tiresome, held strange views upon America, and was more than a little odd. But he seemed at last a model minister for that Patriot King who was to "espouse no party . . . but govern like the common father of his people"; and within ten weeks the Whigs were out, and his eager sovereign, taking Pitt fatally at his word and confident that he "will zealously give his aid towards destroying all party distinctions," watched with his large, unwinking eyes the old man bending low over his hand.

It was from the first a tragic business. One seems to see Pitt's last ministry through a thickening air of failure as his Hundred Days. It opens with the same desperate improvisation; it ends in the same silence of defeat. At the outset a failing man in a perpetual fever assembled his colleagues, that singular array which provoked Mr. Burke to his riot of metaphorical joinery. An Earl of principle was "whimsically dovetailed" with a broad-minded Duke; a sound lawyer was worked into the pattern somewhere; and the dull surface of his Treasury Bench was richly inlaid with the iridescence of Charles Townshend . . . "here a bit of black stone and there a bit of white. . . ." The party system was challenged by a miscellany which nothing but its leader's name could render acceptable; and, with the sudden gesture of a tired man, he changed it. A loyal ballad-monger might complain that

> The Tories, 'od rat 'em,
>   Abuse my Lord Chatham,
> For what—for commencing a peer.

Yet their emotion was not surprising. For Pitt in 1766 was still popular, a reigning toast. But who was Chatham? A new peer, a stranger who accepted favours from the King and had an irritating tendency

> To be America's nabob, sir.

With a strange diminution of popularity he took charge of the country; and for five months he steered his own course with a firm touch. Guns, frigates, Continental allies, and the corn supply made an agreeable tumult in his mind, whilst eager colleagues crowded round Privy Seal with pens and paper to take his Olympian decisions, and Townshend walked out of Cabinet muttering, "What inferior animals the rest of us appear."

But before the year was out he was becalmed; the great vessel lay on the water, and there was scarcely a movement. The world went on; brisk Mr. Townshend settled the affairs of India, sparkled through his "champagne speech," and devised a most ingenious tax on tea in American ports. It was, for Colonial affairs, a fatal interlude. But Privy Seal lay at Bath; sometimes he muttered to a friend by the bedside, sometimes he dictated a majestic note for ministers to a lady with anxious eyes. Once he got as far as London and crouched in a dim room at Hampstead, where a scared colleague saw a huddled figure bowed over a table. He still hoped to work, to see the King, to meet his Cabinet. But soon it was the eclipse. He sat for days alone, starting at sounds, staring at quiet fields in Hampstead. He took little solitary meals at irregular hours, and craved for silence. Across the sea America was strangely disordered. But Privy Seal sat in his little room, gripping a table; his hands were always on the table, and his head was on his hands. His sad-eyed lady wrote his letters, faced the world, kept the house hushed for him, and came when he rapped his stick on the floor. He was quite gone now, and she acted for him under his power of attorney; they say that when he signed, he sang a little. The dreadful time trailed on; until at last they let him resign, and his Hundred Days were over.

In the last phase (for he recovered) he was irregularly seen, like one at a great distance. The voice came faintly down the wind and was lost again. He was like a storm still muttering below the skyline. Once he came to Court and scared his sovereign by his resurrection. Ministers, in full cry after Mr. Wilkes, heard the blind tapping of a familiar crutch and looked nervously behind them. The House of Lords was startled by a hollow voice, which spoke about Magna Carta and "those iron barons—for so I may call them when compared with the silken barons of modern days." He seemed to have his strength again, spoke night after night, and drove past Mr. Burke's at Beaconsfield in a tandem, followed by twenty servants and his family in two coaches and six. Then, remembering how he had once been called "Mr. Secretary Cortez," he scented

some distant impertinence of Spain in the South
Atlantic and swooped like an eagle. He deferred
with elaborate irony to "Spanish punctilios, indeed!"
and woke strange echoes of the Seven Years' War.
But the clouds drifted down again; and when the
mountain was seen through another rift, he was
writing verses to Mr. Garrick upon the pleasures of
the country. He rode, bred pigs, and chartered
Sir Joshua to paint all his friends for the ball-room.
But he still seemed to watch America, where Lord
North was reaping the dismal harvest sown by
Mr. Townshend when Privy Seal lay mute at Bath.
He made deep-chested speeches upon liberty and
taxation and the duty to "proceed like a kind and
affectionate parent over a child whom he tenderly
loves; and, instead of these harsh and severe proceedings, pass an amnesty on all their youthful
errors"; he begged ministers to withdraw the troops
and drafted plans of conciliation with Dr. Franklin.
But the niceties of American jurisprudence were
beginning to concern him less than the menace of
France. That perpetual danger (had he not conducted the French war?) haunted his mind, and he
flung a warning arm to where "France, like a vulture,
is hovering over the British Empire, hungrily watching the prey that she is only waiting for the right
moment to pounce upon." Then the night closed in

again, and for two years (except for a dying state-
ment of his political faith dictated to the doctor, to
whose heroic prescription of Hock, port, and Madeira,
unaccompanied by exercise, he owed, perhaps, the
continuance of his malady) the world went on without him.

Seen for the last time, he passed magnificently
from the shadows into the lighted centre of the stage;
and the melody, which had trailed so long in minor
keys, seemed to sweep into the major. He was breaking fast. But he found his voice again, and as the
Lords strained to hear, he spoke less like an ex-min-
ister than as the Chorus of a tragedy. The hollow
voice comes faintly from those last debates, with its
dreadful burden of doomed fleets and defeated armies
. . . "an end to this country . . . you cannot conquer
. . . driving them before me with this crutch . . .
traffic and barter with every little pitiful German
prince that sells and sends his subjects to the shambles
of a foreign prince . . . the tomahawk and scalping
knife of the savage . . . my Lords, if I were an American as I am an Englishman, while a foreign troop was
landed in my country, I never would lay down my
arms—never—"(one can almost catch the old man's
gasping emphasis) "never—never." He thundered
and lightened; but still the war went on. On the
last day of all he staggered to his place held up

between two young men, like a dying prophet. The voice was very faint now. But he was still speaking, and his mind seemed to dwell on the old danger across the Channel . . . "an ignominious surrender . . . prostrate before the House of Bourbon . . . if we must fall, let us fall like men." It died away. A Duke was speaking. Then the old man stirred and fell back with his last speech strangled in his throat. So he died, almost in public; he could not, one feels, have planned it better. For his death, like his life and his opinions, was magnificently obvious.

THE RIGHT HON. EDMUND BURKE

> *I think it will be found that the grand style arises in poetry, when a noble nature, poetically gifted, treats with simplicity or with severity a serious subject.*—LAST WORDS ON TRANSLATING HOMER.

THE RIGHT HON. EDMUND BURKE

ONE is always tempted to treat Mr. Burke rather as
an anthology than an oracle. That echoing prose
holds the full music of his time. It is the oratorio of
politics—sometimes the plaintive solo, sometimes the
grand chorale. But these thunders and this fluting
are not, one feels, the chosen vehicle of wisdom.
Sages are commonly less melodious. Yet Mr. Burke
was incomparably wise. Truth, eschewing meretricious aids, infrequently resides in a style.
Mr. Burke, when all is said, was a style, a rich, a
shapely and exuberant style. It became, in course
of time, the classical idiom of English politics, the
admired dialect of Honourable and Right Honourable gentlemen. Statesmen, in frequent flight from
definite assertion, have vanished through those endless arcades of eloquence, down that long perspective
so peculiarly friendly to concealment. For the formal
manner is at its best when it is saying nothing. The
slow magic of its touch can make a pronouncement
out of a platitude. Perhaps those balanced clauses
leave it a little difficult on occasion to know when to

cheer. But the effect is infallibly most impressive.
The lesson (since it is obvious) has been widely
learnt. Countless public men in difficulties oblige
with an imperfect recollection of the *Reflections*.
The *pastiche*, it must be confessed, is not uniformly
successful. They do not always catch the style.
Certain requirements of grace and rhythm are not
invariably fulfilled; and often when they hope to
bend the bow of Mr. Burke, they merely discharge
the blunderbuss of Dr. Johnson. But for a hundred
years our public life was conducted in the dying
echoes of that style. Such wide appreciation has
been, perhaps, inimical to his fame. The school is
sometimes apt to obscure the master; and his more
meaningless disciples inspire a faint suspicion of his own
meaning. Those echoes sound a trifle hollow; and
in sharp misgiving one inclines a modern ear. Can
wisdom be so eloquent? Should it turn a sentence
so? Has it, ought it to have a style? One notes his
deep melody and his perfect form with growing
anxiety. For our own tastes are more austere—or
more illiterate. We have learnt to dissociate sound
from sense, to expect our instruction in unpalatable
forms, to mistrust a style; and Mr. Burke, when all
is said, was a style.

But a graver cause impedes appreciation. He
lives, for most of us, in the elusive form of quoted

Burke, 1780

From the picture by Sir Joshua Reynolds in the National Portrait Gallery (from a
photograph by Emery Walker)

fragments, suffering the sad destiny of Quintilian and La Rochefoucauld. For he is disastrously quotable. One sentence lends profundity to a whole speech, and his seven thousand pages are the favourite quarry of hurried public speakers. The workings, strangely enough, are not inconveniently crowded with busy excavators; since a marmoreal passage, once extracted, does frequent duty, ensuring veneration for his quoted name rather than any wide acquaintance with his writings. Have not a thousand orators enquired whether you have a right to make your people miserable or whether it is not your interest to make them happy, stating at the same time their ignorance of the method of drawing up an indictment against a whole people? Do not all visitors to Versailles recall with sensibility how they first saw the Queen just above the horizon, decorating and cheering the elevated sphere she just began to move in, glittering like the morning star, full of life and splendour and joy? Constant quotation tends to obscure him, as frequent fingering blurs the sharp outline of a medal. It renders his page, when read at last, disappointingly familiar. For it is vaguely distressing to proceed through a long succession of *Elegant Extracts*, to study a complete mosaic of prize declamations, here a bit of black stone, and there a bit of white, patriots and courtiers, King's friends and . . . how grossly infectious the habit is. One could forgive him a century of quotations. But the disaster to his fame lies in the most disturbing fact that he is almost equally quotable by both sides; and whilst progressive persons compel applause with his bold surmise that in all disputes between them and their rulers the presumption is at least upon a par in favour of the people, a more somnolent cheer from the opposite party must greet his evocation of the proud Keep of Windsor, rising in the majesty of proportion, and girt with the double belt of its kindred and coeval towers.

This strange duality offers an awkward impediment to his admirers. It is rarely advisable for a prophet to deliver more than one message: a second may easily impair his reputation for consistency. This tepid quality is the first (and perhaps the only) virtue demanded of public characters. Having once mastered their opinions on a single point, we insist that they shall repeat them with increasing emphasis in changing circumstances and upon entirely different topics. They say it; and we cheer. They say that they have said it all before, giving the date; and we wave handkerchiefs. The monotony holds a mysterious power to soothe. Such comfort is sadly wanting in the career of Mr. Burke. For the enlightened Whig of his first manner sharply became a

panic-stricken Tory. His principles, his public utter-
ances, his private friendships were all distorted by
the sudden upheaval. A moment came when his
eloquence seemed to turn upon itself; and his rich
store of progressive sentiments, turned instantane-
ously sour, became a mine of deep reaction. It was
as if he had remembered suddenly that he lived at
Beaconsfield.

He met his first revolution at forty-five with open
arms, and uttered a text-book of constitutional freedom. At sixty he met his second, and turned shuddering away. It was a strange revulsion. And yet
perhaps there were excuses. The challenge of Boston
was aimed at enemies whom he could understand—
at prerogative, at Mr. Townshend, at the exasperating *bonhomie* of Lord North, at the dull eye of
Majesty itself—and he could sympathise. It was a
blameless insurrection, founded on equity and quotations from Blackstone, a sedate rebellion, a sedition
of the highest principles. To sympathise was easy.
For American opinions were the sublime of Whiggery;
and Mr. Burke was Whiggery itself. But France
was scarcely Whiggish; and when Paris throbbed
with the diapason of an angry hive and swarmed
dustily at Versailles beyond the Château railings,
sympathy came less easily to Mr. Burke. For the
challenge of Paris was pointed at government, at

reason and the ordered sweetness of life. It was a roar of hoarse assertion across the quiet voices, a surge of torches into the candle-light. Mr. Burke had respected, had even shared the prim convictions of indignant colonists. But disordered foreigners, who mistook confused ejaculations for public doctrine, were unspeakably disturbing. Their style was lamentable, their principles unworthy, and their loud incoherence distasteful in the last degree. They were not, they certainly were not Whiggish in the least. One could hardly think of persons less likely to be congenial to Lord Rockingham. Rebels, who knew their place, walked by the clear light of reason. Then one might hope to meet them, like Dr. Franklin, at Mrs. Howe's in Grafton Street. But these directed their eccentric progress by a confused and intermittent glare, that troubled English eyes. There was a strange glow on the sky over Paris; and as it reddened, the century turned slowly to its flushed and stormy evening. The sun, the decorously gilded sun of the Eighteenth Century was sinking. There was a sudden chill of night in the air; and Mr. Burke, at sixty, turned shuddering away.

One may forgive his weakness. It was, to all appearance, the end of an age; and he had been far too much the man of it to welcome the cataclysm.

His leaping mind had always worn the sober livery
of its ordered thought; and even in the rich ornament
of his prose he had conformed to its standards. It is
hardly just to measure his wisdom by his failure to
welcome a new world late in life. Silence comes
easily upon peaks in Darien; but when such dis-
coveries invade the watcher's life with threats to all
that has made it gracious or endurable, silence is
scarcely possible. Mr. Burke had lived at the knee
of the Eighteenth Century; and he insisted, with
becoming piety, that it should last for ever. All that
he demanded was a world of ordered freedom, where
manners improved, decorum deepened, and poets
scanned still more strictly. But the note changed
sharply; and Mr. Burke, abhorring the sudden change,
raised hands in commination. If he denounced the
change, at least he denounced it in incomparable
language; and for six years his hearers, yawning
slightly, listened to a sonorous excommunication of
the Nineteenth by the Eighteenth Century.

His claim to sagacity rests on an earlier phase.
Old men in anxious flight from change earn little
more than pity. But twenty years before he had
presented a more estimable figure — a younger
Mr. Burke, still spectacled, but brisker now and
speaking in his quick Irish voice, "never unwilling"
(as Johnson remembered him) "to begin to talk, nor

in haste to leave off." This more youthful person had a pen, a turn of wit, and a secretaryship to Lord Rockingham. That nobleman, one of those singular blends in which our public life abounds, of political rectitude with the Turf, was newly become first minister and viewed the Colonies with well-bred concern. These fractious and remote dependents were recently convulsed (it was the year 1765) by a Stamp Act of Mr. Grenville's. Great gentlemen took counsel with Mr. Burke upon their policy; and, faintly gratified, Mr. Burke assumed their guidance. He guided them for thirteen months by the unwavering light of his principles. He was a Rockingham; and the principles of the Rockinghams were like precious and very fragile china. Applied to America, they showed an easy answer to the riddle. The Stamp Act, since it was Mr. Grenville's, was clearly wrong. So the avenging Rockinghams repealed it with a bright conscience; and half England was reproved. But they were equally convinced that the right to tax reposed in Parliament. The Colonies, in heat, had denied it; and when the Rockinghams asserted the empty right in the Declaratory Act, the Colonies stood reproved as well. So, by the principles of Mr. Burke, the tax was wrong, though it was right to tax. This exacting syllogism represented the policy of Lord Rockingham. It satisfied

134

the blameless craving of his group to be more right than both sides to the quarrel; and, stranger still, it satisfied the Colonies.

This somewhat imperfect contribution to the controversy stands to the credit of Mr. Burke. Later, when discontent was deepening into rebellion, he set to his lips the incomparable trumpet of his style and blew. The call, it must be confessed, found fewer hearers in 1774 than it has quickened since. He fluted to them of "so paltry a sum as threepence in the eyes of a financier, so insignificant an article as tea in the eyes of a philosopher." He thundered to them of Mr. Hampden, or that unforgettable "piece of diversified Mosaick," and of the golden setting of Lord Chatham before the gibbous rise of Mr. Townshend—"Even then, Sir, even before this splendid orb was entirely set, and while the western horizon was in a blaze with his descending glory, on the opposite quarter of the heavens arose another luminary, and, for his hour, became lord of the ascendant." But when he reached the point on which the quarrel turned, he was almost airy—"Leave America, if she has taxable matter in her, to tax herself. I am not here going into the distinctions of rights, nor attempting to mark their boundaries. I do not enter into these metaphysical distinctions; I hate the very sound of them." This was a strange position for the

philosopher of the Rockinghams.   But Britons are
frequently unfriendly to theory; and Mr. Burke, for
all his brogue, was admirably, incorrigibly British.
He exposed a fine scorn of doctrines, a rich contempt
for logical abstractions.   Indeed, it was advisable, if
he was to defend the sanctity of their eccentric system—"the system of 1766. . . .   Until you come
back to that system, there will be no peace for England."   For this mystic combination of the right to
tax with non-taxation still engaged his affections;
and questions of sovereignty were very reasonably
consigned "to the schools, for only there they may
be discussed with safety," whilst he argued that the
power to tax, non-existent in normal times, leapt into
being at the first hint of a public emergency—"no
ordinary power; nor ever used in the first instance.
This is what I meant, when I have said at various
times, that I consider the power of taxing in parliament as an instrument of Empire, and not as a means
of supply."   Such nicety seemed to require an act of
faith rather than any intellectual process.

In the next year his voice rose a key higher.   He
spoke of liberty and "our Gothick ancestors"; he
alluded to law and "the mysterious virtue of wax
and parchment"; he stated, first of a long line, his
ignorance of "the method of drawing up an indictment against an whole people."   He waved the

question of taxation out of sight and soared at large in the free empyrean of abstract liberty, where all precedents would be made one in a purer air above "your registers and your bonds, your affidavits and your sufferances, your cockets and your clearances." In this exalted mood he moved—"I now (*quod felix faustumque sit*) lay the first stone of the temple of peace, and I move you"—the resolutions for conciliation with the Colonies; and an adverse House passed gleefully to the previous question. Restored to earth, he passed uneasy years in a world that obstinately failed to see the complex charms of the settlement of 1766; and in an endless night lit by the red gleams of musketry he wrung eloquent but ineffectual hands, "whilst the liberal government of this free nation is supported by the hireling sword of German boors and vassals, and three millions of the subjects of Great Britain are seeking for protection to English privileges in the arms of France."

Such, in rough outline, was the constructive contribution of Mr. Burke to his first revolution. Unlike his second, it did not scare him into hostile transports. But it elicited the queer medley of 1766; and that entanglement involved him in a perpetual effort to reconcile its oddities with his instinct for freedom. He became, in the outcome, more American than the English and far more English than the

137

Americans. Perhaps the truth reposes in such unhappy amalgams; but they rarely engage the affections of large bodies of men. So he remained a lonely figure, ingeminating woe. That his predictions were fulfilled rendered them still more distastful: for nothing can be more disobliging than a Cassandra who survives the event. His voice still echoed on—"calamity, disgrace, and downfall . . . general blindness of the nation . . . that public storm . . . fall of the first power in the world . . . defeat and shame . . ." And, as it died away, "miserable distraction . . . I have read the book of life for a long time, and I have read other books a little . . . what shadows we are, and what shadows we pursue . . ." Perhaps such voices are created far more for crying in the wilderness than for persuasion. Rarely leaders of their time, these lonely figures are justly the admired of posterity.

So Mr. Burke becomes at last an anthology rather than an oracle, an echoing corridor where the receding voices of the Eighteenth Century may still be faintly heard. One catches them even in the *Vindication*, with its neatly powdered history, its *Odi profanum*— "I do not write to the vulgar nor to that which only governs the vulgar, their passions —," its elegant distaste for "enthusiastical nonsense" and for the obscurities of law, "uncertain even to the professors, an Egyptian darkness to the rest of mankind," with the slightly mincing irony of its "yet another farthing candle to supply the deficiencies of the sun," and its urbane analysis of "the mystery of murder, from the first rude essays of clubs and stones, to the present perfection of gunnery, cannoneering, bombarding, mining, and all those species of artificial, learned, and refined cruelty, in which we are now so expert, and which make a principal part of what politicians have taught us to believe is our principal glory." The note was still clearer in the *Philosophical Enquiry into the Origin of our Ideas of the Sublime and Beautiful.* What other age could have embarked a young gentleman on that enquiry? True to its temper, he observed the sea with mild alarm—"the ocean is an object of no small terror"—and he prescribed for architecture an elegant blankness, having observed that "there is nothing more prejudicial to the grandeur of buildings than to abound in angles." Without pretending to "lay down rules for caprice and to set up for a legislator of whims and fancies," he examined the elements of taste with laudable precision. Beauty revealed her secrets to this ardent searcher, Beauty *à la mode* whose subdued colouring had not yet been drowned in Mr. Lovat Fraser's paint-pot. She charmed by smoothness, fragility—"an air of robust-

ness and strength is very prejudicial to beauty"—
and those faint colours which "must not be of the
strongest kind." Thus Mr. Burke pursued the
Beautiful, keeping a watchful eye on the Sublime.
In the *Observations on a late Publication entitled "The
Present State of the Nation"* the prince approached
his kingdom. With a scornful fling at "the light
squadrons of occasional pamphlets and flying sheets,"
he drove straight at his favourite point, that "politics
ought to be adjusted not to human reasonings but
to human nature." The phrases went off like
crackers—"The prayers of politicians may sometimes
be sincere," and "A man is generally rendered somewhat a worse reasoner for having been a minister,"
and that timeless evocation of Protectionist ideals,
"A teasing custom-house and a multiplicity of per-
plexing regulations ever have, and ever will appear,
the masterpiece of finance to people of narrow views;
as a paper against smuggling, and the importation of
French finery, never fails of furnishing a very popular column in a newspaper." In the next year he was
triumphantly installed, wielding his prose like a
sceptre. The *Present Discontents* scaled every tone,
from the light irony of "It is an affair of vulgar and
puerile malignity to imagine that every statesman is
of course corrupt," to the level wisdom of "Party is
a body of men united for promoting by their joint

endeavours the national interest upon some particular principle in which they are all agreed," and "It is no inconsiderable part of wisdom to know how much of an evil ought to be tolerated." The flame burned higher on *American Taxation;* and the long plea for conciliation showed his steady light—"Obedience is what makes government and not the names by which it is called," and "A great empire and little minds go ill together," and "There are critical moments in the fortune of all states when they who are too weak to contribute to your prosperity may be strong enough to complete your ruin." He saw America; he foresaw Ireland. And, grasping the roots of English policy—"All government is founded on compromise and barter"—he even mastered the more elusive formula of the British Empire, "a wise and salutary neglect."

Then he was off on *Œconomical Reform,* baying the sinecurists, confronting the Treasury with "the grand and sure paymaster, Death," and uttering that deep-chested repudiation, "The calumny is fitter to be scrawled with the midnight chalk of incendiaries with 'No popery' on walls and doors of devoted houses than to be mentioned in any civilised company." India called out his richest tones—"Mr. Hastings feasts in the dark; Mr. Hastings feasts

alone; Mr. Hastings feasts like a wild beast" . . .
He ran through every note in the scale, from the
towering scorn of "Lofty, my Lords!" to the elaborate humility of "I am a man of a slow, laborious,
inquisitive temper." There was assorted wisdom
on every topic, on Cabinets—"There is a sacred veil
to be drawn over the beginnings of all governments";
on judges—"The first and foundation of all judicial
virtues, judicial patience"; on history—"Historians
are generally very liberal of their information concerning everything but what we ought to be very
anxious to know"; on criminals—"Thank God, my
Lords, men that are greatly guilty are never wise";
on departmental committees—"In the obscure and
silent gulph of this committee everything is now
buried." He reprobated "this heroick sharper"; he
denounced "a common dog-trot fraud"; he manufactured the wildest merriment from "an eccentric
book-keeper, a Pindarick accountant." His political
wisdom was exposed in a distaste for "those treach-
erous expedients called moderate measures," his
Parliamentary instincts in "This objection against
party is a party objection," and his resounding
scorn, that still hangs about the roof-beams of Westminster Hall, in "You ought never to conclude that
a man must necessarily be innoxious because he is in
other respects insignificant."

But, as the echoes died away, he was still mouthing his detestation of the horror across the Channel. He had loathed it in the bright dawn of 1789 for its "political theologians and theological politicians" and its horrid suggestion of Cromwell, "one of the great bad men of the old stamp." He hated its clatter—"half-a-dozen grasshoppers under a fern"—and judged it grimly by "conduct, the only language that rarely lies." He found, with grave distaste, "a college of armed fanatics for the propagation of the principles of assassination, robbery, rebellion, fraud, faction, oppression, and impiety" and, faced with the copious outpourings of its theory, curtly replied that "bears are not philosophers." His loathing deepened, as this dreadful object began to "spawn a hydra of wild republics"; and he clung in panic to the protecting battlements of Windsor Castle, "the British Sion." Beyond the sea an odious heresy was insidiously propagated in newspapers—"they are a part of the reading of all, they are the whole of the reading of the far greater number. . . . Let us only suffer any person to tell us his story morning and evening but for one twelvemonth, and he will become our master." The old reformer confessed without shame to "some square-toed predilection for the fashions of our youth," when he was confronted with a Walpurgis of insane philosophers, a cold nightmare

143

of arid theorists—"nothing can be conceived more hard than the heart of a thoroughbred metaphysician." Peace with this thundercloud was unthinkable. It veered; it changed its shape. But always behind it he saw the grinning mask of anarchy— "what signifies the cutting and shuffling of Cards, while the Pack still remains the same?" The outlines varied; but Mr. Burke was implacable. Each change provoked a fresh transport of contempt, until he swept down in thunder on the resourceful Abbé's stock of preposterous constitutions, "ready-made, ticketed, sorted and numbered; suited to every season and every fancy; some with the top of the pattern at the bottom, and some with the bottom at the top; some plain, some flowered; some distinguished for their simplicity, others for their complexity; some of blood colour; some of *boue de Paris;* some with directories, others without a direction; some with councils of elders and councils of youngsters, some without any council at all. Some where the electors cho,se the representatives; others, where the representatives choose the electors. . . ." He thundered on, and still we listen. For Mr. Burke, when all is said, was a style.

LIEUTENANT-GENERAL JOHN BURGOYNE

As for me, the dramatist, I smile, and lead the conversation back to Burgoyne.—NOTES TO THE DEVIL'S DISCIPLE.

LIEUTENANT-GENERAL JOHN BURGOYNE

Iᴛ is the darling error of patriotic persons that history
is made by victories. Handy for perorations, this
view enjoys a wide and natural popularity with public
speakers, writers of stirring ballads, and sculptors
whose talents lie in a memorial direction. It gratifies
the national pride, fits quite compactly into school
textbooks, and is convenient for anniversaries. But
is it more than an agreeable half-truth? Viewed,
indeed, in a colder light, there is far more truth in its
other half. For it takes two sides to make a victory.
The decisive battles of the world have also been
defeats; and possibly the unsuccessful generals are
the true makers of history. A Colonel Weyrother,
unknown to the grateful memory of France, caused
Austerlitz. Bazaine and Benedek made Moltke's
victories. Without the divine ineptitude of Mack at
Austrian headquarters Ulm could never have been a
French triumph; and Villeneuve powerfully aided
Nelson to win Trafalgar. Such debts, one feels,
have been too long forgotten; and history owes to
these neglected figures an un-*Sieges-allee* where de-

147

feated generals might proudly droop in the attitudes of failure. London, perhaps, has made a slight beginning with her artless column to the Duke of York; but the names of his principal defeats are somehow missing from the base. The design is simple—a modest avenue of rue, some battered laurels, and a double line of statues. Melas, wearing his decorations, should contemplate a marble scroll inscribed *Marengo;* whilst MacMahon, frogged and booted, points a modest forefinger at a bronze map of the country round Sedan, and—every inch a Duke— Medina Sidonia stands superb upon a pedestal which reads *Armada, 1588.* For this splendid company made history by defeat: even Napoleon might claim admission on the strength of Waterloo.

In such a revaluation wars assume a different aspect. Strange figures mount new pedestals to claim historic credit; honours are twitched from familiar coats and pinned in unexpected places; and victors change wreaths with vanquished, like hats in a holiday crowd. Harold becomes the hero of the Norman Conquest; bewildered Austrians create Napoleon; and two embarrassed Englishmen in red coats father, with stiff denials of paternity, the United States. Such pipe-clayed ancestry may seem a trifle disconcerting. But when that war is scrutinised, those States are seen to be the portentous creation of two

148

Burgoyne

From a picture formerly in the possession of Miss Burgoyne at Hampton Court, by
permission of G. Bernard Shaw, Esq.

defeats. So, one feels, two nervous parents of mythology may have stared, proud but apologetic, at a giant child. American independence was decided by two engagements, each ending in the dismal courtesy of a capitulation. The first surrender checked a movement which might have been decisive in the King's favour, and won for the Colonies a European ally. The second surrender, made possible by the ally's naval forces, ended the war. Granted that Yorktown and Saratoga decided the issue, there must be a fresh award of laurels. For Gates and Washington have worn them long enough, and it is time for the bays to gleam upon the brows—equally meritorious, if slightly receding—of Lord Cornwallis and John Burgoyne. Did they not lose the war and found the United States? Few men can have a larger claim upon the gratitude of posterity. But posterity, so prodigal of statues, cannot easily find theirs.

It is no pedantry to trace the decision to those two turning points. The failure of the march on Albany in '77 exhausted the first British effort and brought in the French. The Congress might besiege Versailles with the eloquence of Mr. Deane, the sober charms of Dr. Franklin. But France, though fine ladies quoted Rousseau and young gentlemen bought swords and slipped away to sea, was coy. M. de Beaumarchais developed an unsuspected talent for

149

gun-running; but his cautious sovereign remained at peace with England. The news of Saratoga changed the scene. When four thousand Englishmen surrendered in the dripping woods by the Hudson, a sudden light broke on the French. Their sympathy ceased sharply to be a fad, and became a policy. Neutrals have many cares; but none, perhaps, is greater than prolonged uncertainty as to which is the winning side. That once established, judicious statesmanship can do the rest. Since the rebellious colonists had helped themselves, France in the humbler *rôle* of Providence would help them also. Such, in a simple view, were the fruits of Saratoga. Burgoyne surrendered; and by the act he proved that the King's troops were not invincible. It caused a sudden thrill, like that which thirty years later ran through Europe at the news of Baylen, when five French brigades surrendered in a hot Spanish valley on a summer day in 1808, and the world began to doubt the Empire. So Burgoyne rode slowly through the trees, handed a sword to Major Gates, late of the 60th Foot, and made possible the United States.

Years before, an engaging subaltern of Dragoons had jingled through the streets of Preston. There was a war, the unending, customary war of some European succession, which trailed obscurely about

the Palatinate; whilst **Mr. Pitt**, in aquiline indigna-
tion, denounced such

> fiddle-faddle
> About a Hessian horse or saddle.

But Munden's Dragoons were detained by the King's
business in the brisk air of Lancashire; and by the
quiet Ribble a young gentleman wheeled with his
troopers or rode sedately to his quarters. The grand-
son of a Baronet, he showed a pair of singularly fine
eyes; he had from Westminster (the fumes of it still
hung about his style) an education in the classics;
and, more important, he had kept (from the same
source) a noble school-friend, heir to the Earl of
Derby. His friend had sisters; and when the cornet
of Dragoons was entertained by the young ladies, he
pistolled one of them with his fine eyes. While
Lady Charlotte fluttered, Burgoyne resolved. It was
an age when young gentlemen expressed their
preferences in the spirited act of elopement; even a
peer had been known to run with a miss. So, whilst
his flushed sovereign amazed the world at Dettingen,
the eager subaltern secured his nymph. The pair
eloped; the Church (but not the Earl) hallowed their
sudden union; and the Stanleys frowned.

True love ran on in Preston, where he got his troop
and Munden's Dragoons still wheeled by the quiet
Ribble. But the runaways, whom parents could not

151

sever, were parted by Mars. Charles Edward Stuart, embodiment of romance, stepped gracefully ashore at Moidart; and as the pipes began to wail in Highland valleys, King George's troops moved stiffly to the conflict. It was the oddest interlude of ballad poetry in the age of the heroic couplet. Munden's Dragoons broke up from Preston, crossed the Scottish border with the northern garrisons, and formed part, without undue enthusiasm, of the mobile defences of Edinburgh. Mobility was, indeed, their *forte*. They were at Coltbridge, where they found the Highlanders one autumn morning in an unpleasant crackle of pistol-shots, and left in a canter for Dunbar. They were at Prestonpans (but not for long), and left at a hand-gallop for Berwick. The recollection of these encounters was still strong in the following year, when they met them once more on Falkirk Muir in a gale of wind, and left with their accustomed promptitude for a more hospitable scene. War, to a subaltern in Munden's Dragoons, must have appeared a confused and unsatisfactory business, consisting mainly of yelling men with broadswords, scared horses, and bewildered troopers.

In peace the army relapsed into its normal tedium. Worse still, it was extremely costly; and since the Stanleys' frown was not perceptibly relaxed, young love was sadly straitened. So Burgoyne resigned his troop and, with the inspiration common to all Englishmen in want of money, went to France. Writs do not cross the Channel; and poverty is somehow more endurable with only foreigners to see it. They lived abroad for seven years, in which he almost mastered the French language, went to Rome, and was painted leaning, as a man of fashion should, against some ruins in a most becoming waistcoat.

But destiny had not reserved this Hercules for a life of ease with his Lydian queen. The receding line of Byng's top-gallants made a pleasant pattern on the sky-line off Minorca; the Prussians with their powdered heads marched stiffly into Saxony behind a king in a faded tunic; and the world settled down agreeably to seven years more of war. The trumpets sounded; and obedient to the call the man of fashion, now almost become a man of taste, rode once again in scarlet with the long lapels of Honeywood's Horse. Mr. Pitt, aquiline as ever and firm in his new resolve to conquer America in Germany, desired to see whether this happy result might not be achieved as well in France. Honeywood's, with some more, were camped in the Isle of Wight; Anson and Hawke hung off the coast; and one summer day they sailed for St. Maloes. Burgoyne and the bold Dragoons burned shipping in the harbour; and then the armada sailed for home. A few weeks later they were in

France again, watching Howe's bomb-ketches throwing shells into the French, whilst an anxious rearguard scrambled down the beach and back into its ships after a dash at Cherbourg. Then he transferred to the solemn shades which echoed to the measured tramp of the Foot Guards. But the squealing fifes and the rattling drums and the slow march in the sunshine at St. James's were not his destiny. He was not born for bayonets and grenades. For his professional heart was with the cavalry. Something of a *sabreur* and conversant with French (were not "the best modern books upon our profession . . . written in that language"?), he was believed to have absorbed during his residence abroad some knowledge of those mysterious troops of Hussars, Uhlans, and *Chevaux Légers*, which pranced alluringly in Continental armies. So, when the mode reached England and they raised some Light Dragoons, Burgoyne was given a command. He endowed his officers with a code of Mosaic thoroughness, not offered "as the orders of a commanding officer, but as the sentiments of a friend." Adverting sternly to the Prussian system "of training men like spaniels, by the stick," he examined with some pride the reasons "why an Englishman will not bear beating so well as the foreigners in question," and reached the conclusion (startling in 1759) "that English soldiers are to be treated as thinking beings." After this strange flight of speculative philosophy it was hardly surprising that the thoughtful colonel disapproved of swearing at the common soldier and enjoined the study of French and mathematics. Indeed, he seemed to favour an alarming versatility in the gentlemen of the Light Dragoons. Engineering was recommended on the ground that "it strongly exercises the mind, and common reading becomes a relaxation after it." He prescribed (for he was a stylist) "the study of our native tongue"; the practice of "taking views from an eminence" was strongly advised; horsemanship was spoken of highly; and even farriery was commended as being "not at all below the attention of a gentleman" in terms of rare humanity, which took account of "the opportunities which will frequently arise of rescuing a noble animal from the hands of an ignorant and cruel blacksmith."

So the encyclopædic colonel jingled by; and as he took his squadrons past at the salute, the new King found a special pleasure in reviewing "Burgoyne's Light Horse," and the vague, protruding eyes wandered in royal pride down their strange equipment—the little tufted helmet, sword, carbine, bayonet, pistol, and trenching tools. Two troops were sent abroad when Keppel raided Belleisle; and Bur-

155

goyne sailed with them, assuaging his wife's anxieties with a set of verses, in which—always the stylist—he undertook to

> tread the hostile ground;
> Though fiery deaths in tempest shower,
> And thousands fall around.

The fiery deaths being kept within reasonable limits, not more than seven hundred fell around. The returning colonel entered Parliament and continued to exercise upon his command those unusual gifts of style which once led him to assure a startled correspondent upon the uninspiring topic of an additional drum for the regimental band that "I have no wish more sincere than that you may apprehend and believe that I mean to profess myself zealous for the honour of the corps in general, and earnest in my inclination to cultivate your acquaintance in particular. I esteem your ardour for the service; I love your ingenuousness; I am sensible of your talents; I welcome your impetuosity." What could be more Ciceronian? It is not, one feels, for nothing that colonels of Dragoons are nurtured at Westminster.

Such eloquence was demonstrably wasted in a northern climate; and when the King of Portugal was carried, mildly protesting, into war, this faint ally was seconded by a British force, and Burgoyne removed to more congenial skies. From the deck of

a troop-ship he saw the little brown forts slide past
along the gleaming Tagus. Cascaes faded into
Belem; and as the river widened in the sunshine, the
little houses climbed the hills, and Lisbon began. He
walked the dusty streets, at midsummer where they
were languidly rebuilding after the great earthquake.
His command was a mixed brigade of Portuguese and
British, in which his liberal notions of discipline were
severely taxed by a climate that seemed to make
the British thirsty and leave the Portuguese inert.
Somewhere to the east a tangential Spanish invasion
trailed inconsequently about the country. The bold
Brigadier made a sudden march through the heat,
galloped his Light Dragoons through a sleepy town
in the summer dawn, scattered a regiment of foot, and
captured three colours with a staff of officers and a
Spanish general of quality, whom he shamefully
misspelt. Such heroism was fully rewarded. The
Orders of the Day were eloquent; a grateful monarch,
safe in the recesses of Belem, sent a diamond ring;
his judicious minister, more economical, returned the
captured flags to their heroic captor. These triumphs
hardly quenched his appetite for glory; for a neat
surprise at Villa Velha increased his laurels. But it
was the hero of Alcantara that returned to a grateful
country, pleading with engaging frankness for sub-
stantive promotion "upon the pretensions of family

157

support.   Upon any other ground, I should blush to
ask it."   For it was, it was beyond a doubt the
Eighteenth Century.

The firing died away; and in the stillness the world
composed itself for peace.   The violins tuned up at
Versailles for their eternal *rigaudon;* and the Prussian
horns veered from a martial to a rustic air, as the
King beat his experienced sword into a ploughshare
and, with unusual thoroughness, harnessed his
gun-teams to the plough.   Even the colonel of
Dragoons declined upon the arts of peace.   The
House of Commons received him, thanked him for
his services abroad, and heard his voice upon those
Indian topics which seem to exercise a peculiar
fascination upon the military intelligence.   But the
senate, where Mr. Pitt, tremendous in Opposition,
denounced a bewildering succession of Catilines,
hardly sufficed to amuse his leisure.   For whilst he
wore the toga, he inclined an attentive ear to the
Muses.   At first he planned an extensive work upon
the late wars and travelled widely in search of material.   He heard the Prussian fifes in Berlin, watched
the slow march of powdered grenadiers, posted into
Saxony, saw Maxen and Kollin, and traced "with
extreme amusement" the line of Frederick's marches.
He even breached the Emperor's orders and, "by a
little intrigue, a good deal of perseverance, and per-

haps more assurance than I ought to boast of," saw the Austrian manœuvres *incognito*, observing a remarkable blunderbuss for use by mounted troops and a new gun-carriage designed to "cross ditches, or pass the most uneven ground without overturning." These marvels were carefully reported with the deep respect customary in British *attachés* at foreign manœuvres. The Prussian discipline—"to sink and degrade all intellectual faculties, and to reduce the man as nearly as possible to mere machinery"—was still distasteful. But he reflected wisely that methods, grossly unsuited to patriotic drill-grounds, were more excusable in barrack-squares "filled up, perhaps more than a third part, with strangers, deserters, prisoners and enemies of various countries, languages, and religions." His observations were confided to professional friends, and even to Chatham. But the great work was never written. For Clio palled upon the accomplished colonel.

The Muse had sisters; and whilst he voted (with rare twinges of independence) in Lord North's lobby, he followed a slighter, livelier figure through the groves. The Muse of comedy in 1774 was sedately jocular. He wooed her *en règle* in five acts and an Epilogue written by Mr. Garrick for Mrs. Abington, to say nothing of a grand dance of Shepherds and Shepherdesses, and a transformation scene discovering the Palace of Celestial Love, and a Prologue in which:

> Now Marybone shines forth to gaping crowds!
> Now Highgate *glitters* from her hill of clouds!
> St. George's Fields, with taste and fashion struck,
> Display Arcadia at the Dog and Duck!
> And Drury Misses . . .
>   . . . reel through midnight damps,
> With Fauns half drunk, and Dryads breaking lamps

The *Maid of the Oaks* was a genteel *epithalamium* for the nuptials of Lord Stanley and Lady Betty Hamilton, an innocuous anecdote in which the characters meander blamelessly through an almost interminable *Fête Champêtre*. There is an intermittent tinkle of mild lyrics upon:

> Maria's wedding day

or the more rousing note of

> Hark Jowler, hark Rover,
> See reynard breaks cover,
> The hunters fly over the ground;

and a delighted company stares at the brilliant figure of Lady Bab Lardoon—"a superior! a phœnix! . . . and the first female gamester of the time." This charmer is the heroine of naughty paragraphs, which hint that "Lady B. L.'s ill-success still continues at the quinze table: it was observed, the same lady appeared yesterday at court in a *riband collier*, having laid aside her *diamond* necklace, as totally bourgeoise and unnecessary for the dress of a woman of fashion." Caught by the rustic spirit, she masquerades as "Philly Nettletop of the Vale," and obligingly provides the plot and a part for Mrs. Abington. The trifle pleased a private audience, and even reached the boards at Drury Lane.

Flushed with this triumph, the happy author wrote a critical preface upon French Opera, Italian Burletta, and the *Comédie larmoyante;* commented justly upon the absurdity of "five or six fellows with fusils presented at a gentleman's head, and their fingers upon the triggers, threatening his life in bass notes, he resisting in tenor, and a wife or daughter throwing herself between them in treble"; and drew a nice distinction between comic opera and musical comedy, appending a choice example of the former, named *The Lord of the Manor.* This morsel, it must be confessed, is a trifle faded. Even the bright colouring of Moll Flagon—"a Soldier's Coat over her Petticoat, a Gin-bottle by her Side, and a short Pipe in her Mouth"—fails to redeem the blameless tedium of the idyll. It has a gleam or so of brightness; and perhaps there is a slight collector's value in its recruiting posters—the lion rampant in a grenadier's cap; the London tailor "with his foot on the neck of the French king"; the boarded prize, with decks awash with punch and gold-dust; and the golden East, where passing nabobs throw "rough diamonds to the young fifers to play at marbles." Some freak of criticism attributed the songs to Mr. Sheridan. Almost equally mysterious is the reputation of his third comedy, which thwarted in sixteen scenes (and a duel in Hyde Park) the vulgar ambitions of an egregious *Heiress* named Alscrip and elicited from Mr. Walpole the unusual tribute of two readings in one day. He found it "the delight of the stage" and "the best modern comedy"; and it presented a riddle, comparable to some in modern letters, by running through ten editions in a single year. Not less remarkable were its effects upon the author's friend, Lord Derby. That nobleman had seen one play of Burgoyne's at his wedding. He saw another, and made the leading lady his second wife. Could Comic Muse receive a neater compliment from any peer?

But the most intrepid feat of the hero of Alcantara was his Shakespearean exploit. In an operatic version he translated *As You Like It* into the more elegant idiom of Mr. Gay. Amiens sings in the forest *affettuoso*, punctuated by "Hunting symphony, *con molto spirito*"; Rosalind announces her bold intentions with the assurance of Lucy Lockit—

LIEUTENANT-GENERAL JOHN BURGOYNE

In manly vest when I'm arrayed
My air shall hide the timid maid,
With martial arm my spear I'll wield
And innocence shall form my shield.

Indeed, when she sings that

The face that enchants, too commonly wants
The merits that spring from the mind,

the pleasant jigging has effectually drowned her
Gothic original. The world, one feels, must surely
have applauded, had the lyrical Dragoon printed
his opera and made Shakespeare almost modish.
Yet the piece was never played; and he remained
content with the public raptures excited by *The
Heiress*. But before that happy moment arrived,
Burgoyne with his sense of style and his fine eyes,
had ridden into history and out of it again.

A somewhat boisterous candidate, he marched his
freemen to the poll at Preston with a pair of loaded
pistols. The pistol, indeed, appeared to be his
favourite argument in the constituency; but his
demeanour in the House hardly lived up to these
heroic standards. He spoke sedately upon the affairs
of the East India Company, referred with rare en-
lightenment to "the distresses of fifteen millions
of people," and was stern with Lord Clive. But
Whiggish on Indian questions, he was soundly Tory

163

upon America, regarding that fretful dependency "as our child, which we have already spoilt by too much indulgence . . . I apprehend that it is the right of taxation which they dispute and not the tax. It is the independence of that country upon the legislation of this for which they contend." The General found "a charm in the very wanderings and dreams of liberty that disarms an Englishman," but was prepared to exorcise it, if a suitable command could be found. Ministers were discreetly flattering. Mr. Jenkinson gave a look; Lord North gave a nod; and duty called. So the war opened, and irreverent Bostonians sang:

> Behold the Cerberus the Atlantic plough
> Her precious cargo, Burgoyne, Clinton, Howe.
> Bow, wow, wow!

He sailed without enthusiasm in the wake of two senior generals, leaving a wife in failing health. In case of his death, a moving letter commended her to the King. For once more Mars parted the runaways, and once more with poor results.

He watched the smoke of Bunker's Hill from an outlying battery and soon depressed a minister with a judicious appreciation: "Look, my Lord, upon the country near Boston—it is all fortification. Driven from one hill, you will see the enemy continually entrenched upon the next; and every step we move

164

must be the slow step of a siege . . . Count our numbers, my Lord; any officer will tell you . . ." It was a gloomy forecast, dimly relieved by a faint prospect of success (how faint Burgoyne was soon to know) for a combined operation along the line of the Hudson. But his pen was busy with suggestions for discreet negotiation. He even favoured the purchase of General Lee, one of the paladins of Villa Velha, who had recurred in the rebel army. This simple-minded project was blandly opened in a letter to Lord North. Money should not be mentioned crudely, although integrity was "a point in which many a man fancies he possesses more than he really does"; but the public interest, the bright example of General Monk, and even a free pardon might be lightly touched upon. For soldiers, careful of their own and even of their enemies' honour, are rarely sensitive to that of men whom they regard as renegades. His gifts of style found ampler employment in the composition of a hoarse proclamation of martial law and a tremendous letter to General Washington upon the treatment of prisoners. It was a sustained peroration in that Asiatic manner which inspired the irreverent Mr. Walpole to call the author "General Hurlothrumbo." But staff duties in Boston—"to see that the soldiers boiled their kettles regularly"—even when varied by holding the pen for General Gage, were an unsatisfactory occupation; and, with obvious relief, he wintered in England.

His wife was failing fast. Even the King made gracious enquiries; and all that year, after they parted, Burgoyne campaigned in Canada, waiting for bad news. He came home at Christmas to an empty house in Hertford Street, and dragged off to Bath for a cure. But his views upon current strategy had been embodied in a Cabinet paper, which exercised the mature intelligences of his sovereign and Lord George Germaine. It was the old design, which had haunted him since Bunker's Hill—the Revolution cut in half by the line of the Hudson, a punctual meeting of two British armies marching from north and south on Albany. Such things may happen at manœuvres; but they are rare in forest warfare. Yet the King approved; the War Office drew precise instructions for the conduct of a campaign in forests three thousand miles away; and Burgoyne sailed for Canada with orders to meet Howe at Albany. By a slight omission the corresponding orders were not sent to Howe. For orders, by the pleasing ritual of the War Office, required the signature of Lord George Germaine. One day Lord George, on his way to Kent, looked in at the office to perform this arduous duty. The draft was not completed. So Lord George went down into the country and lost America.

That year the rain fell early in the forests. Burgoyne moved down from Canada to the loud accompaniment of a proclamation in his most deep-chested manner. He alluded to the tyranny of Congress, to "the breasts of Suffering Thousands," and to the agreeable prospect that "every species of provision brought to my camp will be paid for at an equitable rate and in solid Coin"; he indicated with a sterner gesture "the messengers of justice and of wrath"; nor was a reference absent, vague with menace, to his Indians. For the stylist, once so Ciceronian, had his Virgilian moments; and the sudden *Quos ego* was almost irresistible. But the threat was scarcely literal; since he hoped, as he informed the House of Commons, that they would "spread terror without barbarity," and he was positive upon the iniquity of atrocities and promiscuous scalping, when he addressed his allies, in the fatuous idiom habitually adopted for intercourse with backward races, upon their duties to their great father beyond the great lake.

That year the rain fell early. At midsummer he retrieved Ticonderoga; and his sovereign, in most ill-regulated transports, invaded the Queen's room with loud, unkingly cries of "I have beat them, I have beat all the Americans." There was even talk of a red ribbon for Burgoyne. But they moved more slowly now through the dripping trees. The march crept southwards through the forest; and in twenty days Burgoyne built forty bridges and covered twenty miles. But as his panting pioneers drove piles across the marshes and their axes rang in the clearings, there was still no news of General Howe. It was not surprising; since, by the enterprise of Lord George Germaine, he had not his orders. That week, in innocence of Burgoyne groping blindly among the northern trees, his sails passed Sandy Hook, bound for the south. "Now," General Washington wrote in grim surprise, "now let all New England turn on and crush Burgoyne."

The march crept on towards the south. The trees, the interminable trees filed slowly by. But the insurrection hung "like a gathering storm" all round them, and the leaves were falling. Some of his men stumbled into a trap; and twice he fought among the dripping woods. The fine eyes were anxious now, although he took champagne and scandalised a German Baroness by positively flirting with a Commissary's wife. But the slow march was ending; and outside a tent among the fallen leaves at Saratoga it ended, when he offered a sword to Gates in face of two halted armies.

168

That failure, as he rode down to Albany behind the rebels, inspired the French and founded the United States; although in Somerset his countrymen, always impervious to exotic names, at once mistook him for a foreigner and celebrated his capture with appropriate glee. So he rode out of history back to Hertford Street, back to a Committee of the House of Commons, back to the playhouse, back to his Muse; until one day he lay at Westminster "as near as may be" to his wife, under a stone without a name. His plays have faded; and his grave is lost. Even the credit of his one defeat belongs to Lord George Germaine. Poor Hurlothrumbo!

LIEUTENANT-GENERAL EARL CORN-
WALLIS

*We were not fairly beaten, my
lord. No Englishman is ever
fairly beaten.*—SAINT JOAN.

LIEUTENANT-GENERAL EARL CORN-
WALLIS

It was at Baiæ that a shadowy guest in an inimitable
scene called on the Procurator of Judæa, stayed to
supper, even stayed (unlike Pilate, his host) for an
answer to a casual question. Did he, the guest enquired, recall a Galilean of the name of Jesus . . .
Jesus of Nazareth . . . crucified for some offence?
The old man frowned, groped in his memory, put a
vague hand to his head, and answered faintly,
"Jésus? Jésus, de Nazareth? Je ne me rappelle pas."

That exquisite effacement of the past is the perfect
comment of an ironist upon the intelligence of
historical characters. Pilate, one feels, was not alone
in this unawareness of his own significance. Perhaps
his siege of Capri was more to Hudson Lowe than his
six years at St. Helena; and even at St. Helena his
intrepid abolition of slavery without compensation
to the island owners may have meant more to him
than the white face at Longwood. When Cauchon
died, he took more pride in his Canon Law or his
new Lady-chapel at Lisieux than in an arid disputa-

tion with a thick-necked, fair-haired girl at Rouen, who stood awkwardly before him and looked with strange eyes, as she answered in her pleasant country voice. Yet he lives in the world's memory of her. The same deception is oddly universal. Authors mistake their masterpieces; martyrs frequently mis-judge their own importance. A tremendous Doctor, writing in a terrifying certainty of his immortality, secures it only from the watchful note-books which caught his least considered sayings. An Arch-Duke, morganatically married but profoundly serious, must have seemed to himself to earn his monument with a lifetime of slightly irritable industry in the stiff, half Spanish state of the Hofburg. Yet nothing matters of his life except his leaving it in the scared sunshine of a little Bosnian town.

How many figures, faced in Elysium with eager questions upon their supreme achievement, must murmur a vague, unsatisfying *Je ne me rappelle pas.* It is so easy to miss the point of others that one may sometimes be forgiven for missing one's own—the more readily, perhaps, when it was a failure. For we may leave the memory of our failures to other people with perfect confidence. Posterity is never a tactful listener; and that side of our immortality will always be secure. But these omissions often have a simpler cause. Sometimes deliberate, they are due quite

174

Cornwallis

From an anonymous engraving in the British Museum

frequently (Pilate's was such a case) to sheer inadvertence. The poor dears make history and never notice it; or they make it and then, like a posted letter, quite forget it. So it may be conjectured that the big, red-faced Governor-General, sometime Mr. Pitt's Lord-Lieutenant and Commander-in-Chief in Ireland, who sat dreaming on his state barge in the steamy heat of 1805 and watched the flood-water of the Ganges swirling past, remembered India, remembered Dublin Castle and that odd negotiation with Joseph Bonaparte under the lee of Amiens Cathedral where the social tone was set by deplorable republican diplomats with "the dress of mountebanks and the manners of assassins," but had forgotten Yorktown.

Defeated generals are pardonably susceptible upon the subject of the unfortunate manœuvre which lodged them firmly in the history books. Sometimes the mood provokes a frenzied excess of explanation, a flow of highly technical apologetics with an accompaniment of admirable maps and uncharitable reflections on their colleagues. Universal among admirals (a more voluble type), this practice is not unknown after military misadventures. Burgoyne wrote a pamphlet; there is an octavo in which Bazaine lost his battles over again; and Kuropatkin frequently explained himself, but never Mukden. But the more usual recourse of the dispirited heroes is to silence. Benedek never wrote the name of Sadowa; Dupont rarely delighted Restoration drawing-rooms with a full narrative of Baylen; Laing's Nek and Majuba long remained among the less popular topics in exclusive clubs; and General Cope was strangely unfriendly to protracted discussion of Prestonpans.

Cornwallis exercised himself in either mode. He had his explanatory moments. *A Narrative of Lieutenant General Sir Henry Clinton, K. B., relative to his Conduct during part of his command of the King's Troops in North America; Particularly to that which respects the unfortunate Issue of the Campaign in 1781*, provoked him to *An Answer to that part of the Narrative of Lieutenant General Sir Henry Clinton, K. B., which relates to the Conduct of Lieutenant General Earl Cornwallis during the Campaign in North America in the year 1781*. This sturdy commentary, penned in the civilian shades of Mansfield Street, elicited from the *Gentleman's Magazine* a review in which the writer, quoting in a crescendo of commendation from Holy Writ, Shakespeare, and Virgil, opined that the Earl had "made as gallant a defence here as he did at York Town"; although the *Monthly Review* observed a trifle acidly that "the vicissitudes attending the joint operation of detached armies will frequently furnish occasions for ill-humour, that would never have discomposed their minds had their endeavours been crowned with success." There was a brisk interchange of *Observations on some parts of the Answer of Earl Cornwallis,* which left the *Monthly Review* sadly adrift in "much rejoinder, about the times of sending orders, receiving dispatches, producing and withholding letters, etc., which the parties concerned will understand much better than any of their readers," and inspired in the *Gentleman's Magazine* a weary conviction that "nothing is more easy, and at the same time more fallacious, than opinions formed by or from events"; to say nothing of *A Reply* (mysteriously signed "Themistocles" and quoting Quintilian) *to Sir Henry Clinton's Narrative Wherein his numerous errors are pointed out,* and *A Parting Word* (unsigned and quoting Demosthenes) *or, a Summary Review of the Controversy between Sir Henry Clinton and Earl Cornwallis Occasioned by the Observations lately published by that Gentleman on his Lordship's Answer.*

But the debate died down. "These brave but unsuccessful warriors," in the manly phrase of the *Gentleman's Magazine,* pursued their several careers without those penalties which attend failure in the service of more vindictive (or less forgetful) nations. Clinton withdrew with dignity to Gibraltar, glowered with every gun in his command at the Spanish shore, and watched the bulk of Africa across the dancing Straits, as Cornwallis travelled a more varied course. He governed India, made land systems, stormed Seringapatam, and presided imperturbably over sun-dried but voluble subordinates capable at need of minutes in five hundred paragraphs on revenue and rent; he governed Ireland and passed an Act of Union for Mr. Pitt; he went to France and, holding an olive-branch with one hand and his nose with the other, made peace with Buonaparte for Mr. Addington. Somewhere across the world a kindly mist enfolded the low shape of the Yorktown peninsula. It had receded now, revisiting him only in dreams or in that unpleasant vision which once drove the tired negotiator at Amiens to exclaim in a vivid military nightmare, that "I have often wished myself either in the backwoods of America, at 200 miles distance from my supplies, or on the banks of the Caveri, without the means of either using or withdrawing my heavy artillery." The scene had faded—General Washington's hard smile, the pounding drums as the tired men marched out of the battered town to the cheerful air of "The World Turned Upside Down," the dismal ritual of surrender, a dinner, candles on the table, the French in their white tunics, and the

bright eye of La Fayette, toasts of elaborate friend-
liness, and "the illustrious part that your Excellency
. . . long and arduous contest . . . matter of
history . . . laurels." It had all faded now.
Washington was dead and buried somewhere; the
French were centuries away from the King's white
uniforms; La Fayette lay in an Austrian prison;
and as he sat dreaming in the heat of 1805, Cornwallis had forgotten Yorktown.

But Yorktown remains. Faded, perhaps, for him,
it lingers in the world's memory. For the world's
memory works differently. His Act of Union is
repealed; his Peace of Amiens was an ineffectual
interlude; even his Perpetual Settlement of Bengali
tax and tenure somehow lacks perpetuity. But
Yorktown remains, evoking in the memory a line of
crumbling earthworks, the flagging guns, a sudden
silence as the smoke hung in the still, autumn air,
and a big, politely deprecating soldier. For Yorktown, with Saratoga, led in the United States; and
Cornwallis walks down history in that odd *cortège*.

Nature, indeed, appeared to have designed him for
a walking part. Born in Grosvenor Square, he was
baptised yet more conformably with the *ton* at St.
George's, Hanover Square; and from the first he
seemed the very picture of a walking gentleman of
the age. Son of a fifth Baron and first Earl, good

breeding dictated that he should learn his elements at Eton. Even his accidents were of the highest gentility. For when an impulsive hockey-player injured his eye for life, the fatal blow was struck by a future bishop. Enriched with these experiences, he became an ensign in the Foot Guards and travelled on the Continent in search of a military education, accompanied by a Prussian officer who reported his progress in the most abominable French to an anxious parent. The pilgrims, guided by some mysterious predilection, reached a Military Academy at Turin with an eccentric curriculum. Dancing began at dawn, followed by German grammar and riding. A fencing lesson rounded off the morning. The afternoons were less exciting. For a tutor called at three to impart an hour or so of mathematics and fortification; and a final dancing class completed the happy day. Fitted for high command by this terpsichorean training, he joined the staff in Germany and saw the fight at Minden. Recalled to England, he was promoted captain of the Line, came of age, was promptly elected member for the family borough, and commanded a battalion at twenty-two—the very picture of a walking gentleman.

But two years of active service in a marching regiment gave him a more substantial training. He was a soldier now; and when peace seemed to afford

an opportunity of practising the more frivolous items
of the Turin curriculum, he still trailed dutifully
round the garrison-towns with his battalion. At
twenty-seven he was (supreme exile) in Scotland;
the roving colonel saw in his professional pilgrimage
the sad façades of Dublin, the great tower of Gloucester, and even the little shady streets which run
in and out between the Rock and Algeciras Bay. At
twenty-nine, still soldierly, he married a soldier's
orphan. The act, hardly surprising in a colonel, was
almost improbable in an Earl (for he had succeeded
to his earldom). But the warrior was scarcely sub-
merged in the senate, although he attended intermittently to vote with the Whigs and once, more
soldierly than ever, to resist the Cider Tax.

So the walking gentleman, if he ever existed, had
vanished in the assiduous colonel with his parades,
his soldier's orphan, and his distinctly Whiggish
views. Almost a Wilkite, he stood boldly for the
privilege of Members of Parliament to indulge their
proclivity for seditious libel without the incon-
venience of arrest; and his American opinions took
him into the empty lobby where Lord Camden and
Lord Shelburne voted almost alone against the
Declaratory Act. When Chatham came in, the
wild inconsequence of the age of sinecures made
the Whiggish colonel Chief Justice in Eyre South

of Trent; judicial experience was hardly requisite in this ornament of the Bench, since he never sat. Marked for promotion, he next exercised (by deputy) the still less arduous functions of Vice-Treasurer of Ireland. But his ambitions never strayed from his profession. He accumulated dignities as aide-de-camp to the King and Constable of the Tower; and when the restless colonies broke into war, his career, stronger than his convictions, sent him across the sea as Lieutenant-General in America. Untrue to her pedigree, the soldier's orphan would have detained him; and, responsive to her distress, his uncle the Archbishop even interceded with the King. But in '76 he sailed and played a minor part in the opening moves. He came home on leave in '78, but sailed again. She watched the tall ship out of Portsmouth Harbour and trailed back to Suffolk, where she drooped and died. Her soldier left his war again; but the ship sailed slowly, and he never saw her. A melancholy fancy laid her beneath a stone without a name, and by her wish they planted a cruel thorn-tree above her heart.

The widower returned dispiritedly to his command, to a war which he regarded with vague distaste and a commander who showed an alarming tendency to resign in his favour. Few remained out of all the

heroes who had sailed to this interminable siege of
the new Troy. Gage was at home; Howe was revising
his *Narrative;* Burgoyne was back in Hertford Street.
Clinton survived, a trifle querulous and sending his
annual resignation to Lord George Germaine. That
sage, unrivalled organiser of defeat, presided at the
War Office. Familiar to an earlier generation as
Lord George Sackville, he was court-martialled after
Minden, dismissed the service, and expelled the
Privy Council. These awful consequences had attended an unfortunate disobedience to orders whilst
in action. But his country, with its genius (always
warm, and frequently misplaced) for forgiveness,
wiped them all away; and his grateful sovereign, by
whom he had been declared unfit to serve in any
military capacity, appointed him with exquisite ap-
propriateness Secretary of State for the Colonies and
for War. With rare ability he contrived to lose them
both. This spoiled child of defeat projected military
operations for punctual execution three thousand
miles away, enriched them with a bewildering wealth
of wholly inapplicable detail, pelted his generals with
a hail of ill-informed instructions, and watched their
invariable failure with a malign dissatisfaction; until,
these genial auspices presiding over British arms, the
United States sprang fully-armed from the brain of
Lord George Germaine.

Cornwallis, momentarily stifling the resignations of his chief, drifted without enthusiasm into the campaign of 1780. Advancing a trifle ponderously behind the leaping brilliance of Tarleton and his Legion, he marched through South Carolina and at Camden laid a heavy hand on the precarious laurels of Major Gates, late of the Sixtieth Foot. A rapturous Parliament passed grateful resolutions. But his advance was checked, and he passed an unsatisfactory winter. Followed an orgy of cross-purposes, in which the War Office supposed the south secure and reinforced the north, the north in the same delusion planned the evacuation of the south, and the bewildered south, knowing its weakness, moved uncertainly towards the north. This triangle of misunderstanding was maintained by a cross-fire of correspondence between Germaine and Clinton; while in its southern apex Cornwallis abruptly transferred himself two hundred miles to the north, seemed to repent, and passed a tiring summer counter-marching to an exhausting tune played by the more sprightly La Fayette. Growing spent, he backed dispiritedly into Yorktown. The trap closed suddenly—"The enemy's fleet has returned. Two line-of-battle-ships and one frigate lie at the mouth of this river . . . I hear Washington arrived . . . my half-finished works . . . at least six weeks from this day." It came in four weeks—the crumbling earthworks and the flagging guns ("only one eight-inch and little more than a hundred cohorn shells remained") and the hard smile of Washington.

Cornwallis was at his most charming in defeat. He made a graceful speech at table and maintained the exacting *rôle* of an unhorsed but still amiable knight. He borrowed works on tactics from French officers; and when he reached New York on parole, he even remembered in the midst of a pardonably warm debate with Clinton to despatch to Rochambeau a most disarming consignment "*de quelques Fromages et de Porter Anglais, que je vous prie, de me faire l'honneur de m'agréer.*" So the big, easy man emerged from misadventure, and walked once more sedately down the long avenue of his career. It took him back to Suffolk, into the library at Mansfield Street where he read military books imperturbably, to India, to the judicial convolutions of the Perpetual Settlement to Seringapatam, to Dublin in the drizzle of 1799, to the Act of Union, to Amiens and the dark features of Joseph Bonaparte, and back at last to India again, where he sat dreaming in the heat of 1805 with Yorktown quite forgotten.

Yet that campaign, even though his part was slightly passive, remains his most decisive action. For Yorktown, as the phrase goes, made history

185

with rare precision. The outline of decisive battles is frequently blurred by the peace that follows them; the edges of their sharp decision are often blunted by compromise. But no timid adjustments followed Yorktown. Lord North flung up his arms; Germaine resigned; and soon Dr. Franklin was putting his name, with its little flourish, between the pedantic clarity of John Jay and John Adams at the sealed and ribboned foot of a treaty of "firm and perpetual peace" between the United States and a friendly sovereign who reigned in London. The war was over; and as it ended, the United States began.

One sees it, somehow, as a bull-fight, an interminable *corrida* which dragged on for six years. It swayed obscurely across great rivers, along the shores of shining, level lakes, down long defiles where the dark pines gathered for their slow march across the hills. Sometimes it reeled out into the sunshine, and the bayonets gleamed behind yellow sandhills by the Atlantic or in the hot, green fields. But it had always something of the bull-ring. The war had opened as suddenly on the bare hills above Boston as the first bout opens with the quick, angry trot of a big Miura bull into the sunlight. All round them, tier upon tier, the adorable, silly world of the Eighteenth Century sat watching. There was the same hush as he checked, trotted slowly round the ring,

186

caught a vague gleam of cloaks, and cantered heavily—head down, horns up—at his first horse. Trenton and the Brandywine, White Plains and Saratoga were the feints and wheelings of the first movement, which tired him out. Burgoyne's attack was almost brisk. But the British effort failed to lift the whole weight of New England; and it strained as the bull strains under the dreadful burden of horse and rider. He was tiring now; and as the big head began to droop, the barbs were planted and the bright *banderillas* fluttered gaily behind the long horns. Then the last bout opened. A few passes with the red cloth (for La Fayette's campaign was little more), and the tired bull was posed for the *matador*. So, as one seems to see them, the armies came to Yorktown. Then the bright sword plunged; the bull dropped heavily; and the ring was roaring.

GENERAL WASHINGTON

> *Il y a des reproches qui louent,*
> *et des louanges qui médisent.*
> LA ROCHEFOUCAULD.

GENERAL WASHINGTON

IT is, as they say, a wise country that knows its own
father. The floor of history is littered with the
broken toys of fractious nations; but their parents
survive these dire upheavals. Torn flags, dis-
coloured laurels, violated constitutions lie about in
heaps; and sad-eyed historians wade knee-deep in the
wreckage, tidying up the nursery like anxious gover-
nesses after a party. Discarded heroes welter in their
sawdust; patriotic reputations are damaged beyond
repair; and there is a dismal profusion of maimed
heraldic monsters. Leopards and unicorns and sala-
manders limp sadly into limbo; eagles of every
shape—white eagles, eagles in crowns, two-headed
eagles, eagles with thunderbolts, the little Roman
eagle, and the brass eagles of the Empire—flap
heavily after them; and the tiny owls of Athens go
hooting, disconsolate, down the wind. There is even
a faint, receding buzz from a disbanded swarm of
Napoleonic bees. The simpler emblems—Bourbon
lilies, bright Phrygian caps, sunbursts with gleaming

191

rays, Braganza globes, and Tudor roses—are all faded and broken, as the nations outgrow their bright coloured playthings. But their parents are, happily, of a more durable quality.

There is (it has been observed in family life) a permanence about parents. They are not easily outgrown. They do not fluctuate with tastes in toys. They can go out of fashion without going, like humbler objects, out of existence. Enduring with a fine persistence, they provide a constant background and an immutable tradition. Happy, therefore, the nation that knows its parents. The knowledge gives to it a poise, a standing, which are denied to less fortunate races. Its achievement starts from a fixed point, and its splendid growth can be measured by an established standard. It can refer, at need, to the parental tradition; and its lineage may provide by turns a stimulus, a warning, and a boast. No clear analysis has yet been made of the effects of such parentage upon national history. It may emerge that nature sets an indelible stamp of superiority upon the brow of those happy races which know who their father was. Possibly the world is a harder place for foundling nations. Perhaps the Roman owed his victories to a pervading consciousness of Romulus. Conceivably Englishmen, insufficiently aware of Caractacus and Boadicea, with

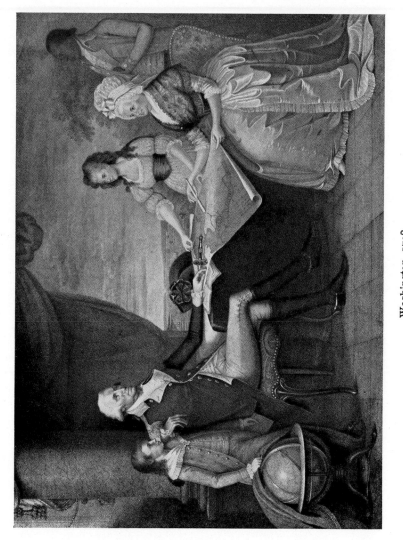

Washington, 1798

From a picture painted and engraved by E. Savage

breasts that rarely thrill to the name of Hengist (or even Horsa), owe the frequent embarrassments of British policy to their distressing lack of a common ancestor. How much simpler, in moments of uncertainty, was the Spartan's direct appeal to the tradition of Lycurgus, the Frenchman's (before Sedan) to Napoleon, or that clear memory of Bolivar which is the somewhat unsteady lodestone of a whole sub-continent. A country with a father seems to steer a more settled course. Its monuments are all the same. Its public speeches all end in the same way, its streets in the same square. Its policy is drawn after a fixed star. For they shine, the fathers of their country, with a cold, perpetual light; and none, in that chilly constellation, with a more unwinking beam than George Washington.

His status is, as it must remain, unchallenged. Father, beyond question, of his country, he sits a little stiffly in that alarming company of the founders of states, with Romulus and the others. Perhaps there are rather too many foreigners about for him to be altogether at ease. Perhaps the big, tilted head was always a little stiff on public occasions—and public occasions are all that remain for him now. No more a romp "with one of the largest girls"; or the exquisite anguish of writing verses (among the frontier surveys in his journal) to his "Lowland

Beauty"; or "that chaste and troublesome passion" for Miss Carey; or the pleasant thrill as Mrs. Washington rolled into camp before Boston behind her black postilions in the white and red. Nothing re-remains now but an eternity in his niche, where the father of his country, so admirably adapted to the exigencies of sculpture, stands frozen in his perpetual attitude. His dignity had always a slightly Chinese immobility. It inspired, perhaps, on the winter day in 1800—when the white ensigns hung at half-mast in the Channel and the First Consul listened with commendable patience to the obituary eloquence of M. de Fontanes—the melancholy tribute of the Celestial Empire. "In devising plans"—there is a grave, unwinking dignity about the Imperial style— "Washington was more decided than Ching Sing or Woo Kwang; in winning a country he was braver than Tsau Tsau or Ling Pi. Wielding his four-footed falchion, he extended the frontiers and refused to accept the Royal Dignity. The sentiments of the Three Dynasties have reappeared in him." At first sight the exquisite grotesques of that stiff embroidery, with which a pedantic patriot has enlivened the more sober homespun of his narrative, are little more than an engaging curio. But as one studies the official Washington, there is a faint, disconcerting dawn of a resemblance. The Washington of parade—the stiff figure once eyed by respectful crowds, driving down to Congress behind the President's white liveries—has something of that immobility as it revisits annually the grateful memory of his countrymen. One seems to see the hand with the big knuckles pointing perpetually at an illegible scroll, or resting eternally upon a sword-hilt. The broad face, with the bleak grey eyes and the heavy jaw and the ill-fitting teeth, which startled Mr. Ackerson of Alexandria, Va., is half forgotten. Anxious historians, familiar with General Washington and President Washington, conduct a desperate search for the missing George Washington. The big angular man, who once danced with the Boston ladies at Governor Shirley's, has almost faded into a gesture of traditional statesmanship; and an awed posterity stares nervously at the tall figure in black velvet which stands *in loco parentis* to one-twentieth of the human race.

But there are certain drawbacks about parentage. The best parents are, oddly enough, the quickest to be forgotten; since a good father is so apt to be replaced in memory by the more shadowy figure of a still better father. Irreverent children frequently retain a precise image of their parents. But a more blameless offspring is rarely equal to this kindly service; since piety, which blurs the vision and impedes the memory, is singularly weak in portraiture.

It seems to prefer to reality the smooth, incredible finish of memorial sculpture, it shrinks from fact into the calmer air of epitaphs. And in the outcome favoured reputations, which might have engaged the reverence of the world, are frequently overwhelmed by their own monumental masonry.

Washington has suffered almost equally from his own qualities and from the piety of his descendants. The father of his country has been deprived of his identity by his grateful children. A worse father might, perhaps, have been more accurately remembered. But the very faultlessness of that singular career seemed to invite the worst that pious ingenuity could do for him. He was encrusted with moral tales which equally repel belief and admiration; his noble figure was draped in the heavy folds of those Teutonic virtues which the Anglo-Saxon imagination erroneously attributes to the Romans; and he became a dismal embodiment, derived in equal parts from the copy book and the political platform, of those public qualities which every nation claims as its private birthright. Never, one feels, has a life of public service been worse rewarded by posterity. He saved, in a military sense he made, the Revolution: and its happy heirs have repaid him with a withered nosegay of schoolgirl virtues. Misconceived panegyric has made him almost ridiculous; and chivalry dictates his rescue from the dull swarms of commonplace with which he has been belittled.

This sad defacement is not the work of envious foreign hands. Whilst he lived, Washington enjoyed a singular freedom from hostile calumny, and after his death his enemies were generous: perhaps it is permissible to remark that his enemies were English. No other race idealises in the same degree those against whom it has fought. One cannot recollect any graceful French tribute to Mr. Pitt or Count von Moltke; Germany still regards Napoleon through the strained eyes of 1813; Italian estimates of Count Radetzky are lamentably deficient in perspective; and even in Spain, so prone to acquiescence, a just appreciation of Bolivar is long overdue. But successful insurrection or victorious warfare against British armies is an unfailing passport to esteem in England. No calendar of her favourite saints is complete without St. Joan; no catalogue of patriots would evoke a single British cheer if it omitted a noble American, a blameless Boer, and an Irish name or so. Allies are scrutinised with a more dubious eye; but enemies receive, almost without distinction, a national tribute. Perhaps it is an inverted form of vanity; perhaps the national greatness requires the attribution (sometimes on slender grounds) of a corresponding greatness to enemies.

But the result in the case of Washington has been singularly happy. One cannot imagine that a biography of Miltiades from Persian sources would exhibit in the same degree his better nature, especially if he had united with his own the more exasperating qualities of Aristides. Yet for Washington British tradition has adopted almost without question the richest embroideries of American myth; and the responsibility for his strange disguise rests solely upon his countrymen. His motives, his simple-minded statesmanship, even his military record have been accepted in England at their face value. The worst enemies of his just appreciation have been his political heirs, the beneficiaries of that lavish testament of freedom; and the problem, if one enters upon the arduous pursuit of truth, is to disengage the figure of Washington from the impenetrable shadow of the cherry tree.

The first essential of sound portraiture is background. The park, the looped velvet curtain, the invariably decisive sea-fight behind him may tell so much about a sitter that is concealed by his impenetrable stare. Yet history, disdainful of significant detail, is lamentably apt to divorce her favourite characters from their surroundings; to present them in a statuesque isolation that is all pedestal and no perspective; to leave them, insulated and gasping for air, in a sort of historical vacuum. Perhaps that is why, in her stately pages, they so rarely contrive to live. Each in his niche, they eke out a dismal and motionless existence. They meet no one except historical characters of equal eminence; and, denied all society except the forced and frequently distasteful associates imposed upon them by historical parallels, they live like solitaries in a sort of historical Thebaid. This harsh treatment, which has become our invariable tribute to true greatness, is singularly misleading in its results; since in separating a great figure from its background we rob it of all perspective, deprive its attitude of meaning, and substitute a majestic effigy for the human figure which once moved in a living scene. Background, the full and accurate rendering of *milieu*, is the first element of historical portraiture; and it is more than usually needed in the case of Washington, if that impassive figure is to be rescued from the dull chisel of the monumental mason and persuaded to live outside the chilly walls of a national Valhalla.

Of all his contemporaries, he is perhaps the easiest to "place." Some men prefer to live uneasily in advance of or comfortably behind the times. But others are unmistakably of their period the "collector's pieces" of history. Chatham might be an alarming *revenant* from the age of Elizabeth; and perhaps the

Methodists oddly anticipate the spiritual quality of the Victorians. But Washington, in outline, and in detail, was purely eighteenth-century. That age, in a higher degree than almost any other, has stamped its products with the mark of their origin. Its prose, its painting, its chair-backs, its poets, its spoons, and its divines were almost uniformly true to period. There is a timelessness about Chartres or the great tower of Marrakesh, a generalised quality about Shakespeare or Velasquez, which might assign them to any age of high achievement. But who could ascribe Mr. Burke to the wrong century? What critic could misdate Sir Joshua, what connoisseur misplace the work of Mr. Chippendale? It is not simple to analyse the common denominator which unites the various achievement of the century. Perhaps it was a pervasion of good manners. Art, strategy, politics, even theology seemed to become exercises in deportment. Polite philosophers aired their courtesy, and accomplished poets displayed their good breeding. Or perhaps the singular uniformity of the age derives only from a certain finish of surface, from an exquisite veneer which coated all its diverse products and lent to each of them a precisely identical gleam. The scene was lighted with a discreet and universal glow, against which a deft troupe of traditional figures—the parson and the squire, the man of leisure and the man of taste, the libertine and the Methodist—performed their grave gyrations. The age, it seemed, was a delightful play with parts for everyone, since all talents could be accommodated with sonorous tragedy, elegant comedy by candle-light, or the broader scenes of life below stairs. Sometimes, perhaps, a person of spirit refused his *rôle* and survived, untrue to his age, a living anachronism. But Washington accepted, and played to perfection, the part of squire.

His rendering of this character, so patient and so complete, appears to distress the more pedantic of his political heirs. They are, somehow, disappointed to find at the head of the triumphant insurrection against King George a figure so exquisitely Georgian. Indeed, for the patriotic *amateur* of heroic contrasts there must be something singularly exasperating in the performance. If only, one feels, he had realised the rich American future—what a gesture he might have made. But the *beau rôle* was irretrievably neglected. Washington obstinately refused to be a picturesque forerunner and clung to his grave decorum. A national hero who declines, however courteously, to oblige with a demonstration of the national characteristics must expect stern treatment. And as the tall, the rather terrifying squire of Mount Vernon moved stiffly through his strange career, he scandalised the more exacting patriotism of unborn observers. For there was something unforgivably, almost defiantly (dare one say?) British in his demeanour which left a loyal posterity with no decent alternative to a drastic repainting of his portrait. It was idle for him to urge in mitigation that civil wars, unhappily, engage upon both sides the same national qualities. Cromwell, he might plead, had been as English as King Charles; and Lee was no less American than Lincoln. But neither of these leaders of revolt founded a nation; and, by an unkind inversion, the father of his country is expected to take after his children. If Washington was at fault in this respect, posterity noted the dereliction and with a silent rebuke removed the traces.

Yet as one uncovers mechanically before the traditional effigy, one parts with a faint regret from the real figure at Mount Vernon, from the solitary old gentleman riding round his farms in the sunshine, with "plain drab clothes, a broad-brimmed white hat, a hickory switch in his hand, and carrying an umbrella with a long staff, which is attached to his saddle-bow." He seems, if one studies him rather among the voices and the colour of his background than in the silent vacuum of history, a living person, who had been so true to class and to period. This unwitting father of a new world rode to hounds with a peer and a peer's brother. A fox-hunting squire in buckskin breeches and a blue coat, he jolted indomitably behind a pack, whose names—Singer and Truelove, Music and Sweetlips—have more of "John Peel" than of the Rights of Man. He led the field on a big grey, while the ladies went round by the road and Mrs. Washington in her scarlet caught a glimpse of his jockey-cap between the trees. The big man once thrashed a poacher with a gusto which would have evoked the sympathy of any Warwickshire bench; and when he rode in to sit with the Burgesses at Williamsburg, this master of hounds might well have been any Justice of the Peace that ever dismounted at a country courthouse to administer a well-bred approximation to the Common Law. On great occasions he rose to rare heights of equestrian elegance, with a family crest displayed at convenient points of his saddlery and a generous profusion of his white-and-scarlet livery in the cavalcade.

And he was no less true to race. Unmoved by the *wanderlust*, which urges his unresting heirs upon their never-ending travels, he passed his long life in one continent, with the solitary distraction of a single excursion to the West Indies. Lacking their fine cosmopolitanism, he was rarely, one feels, at ease in the company of foreigners. So voluble as to be sometimes a little trying to a rather silent gentleman, they were lamentably prone to an excess of flourish in the field. They struck attitudes; they clanked; they looked, as no gentleman ever should, the part. With the exception of a purely technical respect for a competent German or so and a single friendship (and that with a Marquis), they jarred upon a singularly unassuming soldier, who had unlearned all *panache* since the brave Colonial days when Mr. Walpole had described him to Sir Horace Mann as "an excellent fanfaron"; and their more martial demeanour accorded ill with his grave, his perilously British distaste for uniform. In the same mood of unostentation he warned young Custis not to spend a ten-dollar bill on a gown at Princeton, since the classes might "be distinguished by a different insignia . . . otherwise you may be distinguished more by folly, than by the dress." It was a wary piece of counsel which might have been addressed from any manor-house in Leicestershire to any college at Oxford. Foreigners, one recalls, were always making themselves conspicuous; and nothing could be more distasteful. So it is not surprising that a proposal to endow American education with a complete faculty from Geneva elicited grave Presidential fears of a "seminary of foreigners." Wholesale immigration is deplored (the terms would not be unbecoming to a Norfolk magistrate during an influx of Flemings) if the immigrants are to "retain the language, habits and principles, good or bad, which they bring with them. Whereas by an intermixture with our people, they or their descendants get assimilated to our customs, measures and laws; in a word, soon become one people." The long search for a true Americanism seems to start from sentiments which delightfully resemble British insularity expanded to embrace a continent.

He had, like any gentleman of the age, his moments of modish cosmopolitanism, when "I trust you think me so much a citizen of the world as to believe I am not easily warped or led away by attachments merely local and American; yet"—true to race again —"I confess I am not entirely without them, nor does it appear to me that they are unwarrantable, if confined within proper limits." The Anglo-Saxon is rarely equal to an exalted sense of international duty; and when the brotherhood of man appeared in an awkward gleam of French bayonets behind the beating drums of 1793, the President, no less than Mr. Pitt, remembered that brotherhood begins at home. The slow growth of his distaste for the French Revolution is one of the most instructive operations of that ingenuous mind. It cannot, one feels, have alarmed him because it was a revolution, since in his time he had made a revolution himself. But may the fatal cause have been that it was French? Even at the outset, when the thundering fall of the Bastille was still in the air and London was ringing with the shrill jubilation of Mr. Fox, he was guarded in his predictions. As the note deepened in the Place de la Révolution and the French proceeded in their dreadful way to the logical conclusion of their opinions, he drew the hem of the young Republic's garment tightly round her in the ample gesture of neutrality, and passed by. And when the egregious Genêt landed, with his antics and his eloquence and his deplorable style, he was confronted by a bland, a courtly, but an indubitable fragment of the *ancien régime*. Washington was never more completely the Whig gentleman than in his attitude to the French Revolution. He had always worn the blue and buff of a Virginia colonel. Three thousand miles away it was the Whig uniform; and there is so much in his temper that leads one to expect him, when the cloth is removed, to lift a port glass to "Buff and blue, and Mrs. Crewe." Yet he would not, one feels, have followed Mr. Fox. He must surely have applauded the grave, comminatory eloquence of Mr. Burke. He would have denounced regicide with a stern forefinger in the House of Commons; and when the Duke of Portland brought the Whigs over, Mr. Washington would have stood firmly with Mr. Pitt. He might, he must have sat with him in Cabinet. There is nothing incongruous in the combination. One can almost see the big jaw and the black suit on the Treasury Bench, watch the large knuckles on the despatch box, read the measured speech in Hansard. There was nothing in Washington to prevent it. But, born beyond the sea, he became by an alternative destiny the first American (and, perhaps also, the last Englishman) to govern the Thirteen Colonies.

One is far from asserting that George Washington was an Englishman astray in Colonial politics; since it would be rash, as well as tactless, to lodge a British claim to someone else's national hero. His whole achievement was impeccably American. He stood, he fought, he planned for the United States. He was, more truly than most men of whom it is said, the father of his country. But countries have grandparents as well; and as one watches the long shadow of Washington on the wall of history, one is aware of a growing certainty that he took strongly after his mother—after the suave, reserved, well-mannered England of the Eighteenth Century, where unhurried gentlemen, avoiding all parade, sedately undertook their public duties and bowed to one another a little stiffly. He seemed, as it were, to play an American part with the faintest suspicion of an English accent. He saw with a surprising clarity the broad vision of a continent controlled by a single people. Such visions are apt, in other races, to breed visionaries. But perhaps there was a colder, more northern light in the level eyes which saw their vision in terms of sound finance and waterways. Even in his military achievement one sometimes catches a queer echo of his enemies. It is the depressing destiny of British commanders to conduct military operations on behalf of legislative bodies. With an acute sense of their imperfections and a lively resentment of their control, they victoriously extend their boundaries in a mood which must always recall the somewhat uncertain relations of General Washington to Congress. Mr. Walpole might allude with graceful erudition to Fabius and Camillus and the institution of dictatorship. But it was the misfortune of the American dictator, which must engage the sympathy of all British soldiers, that his Senate remained in constant session. Like one of Wellington's fox-hunting brigadiers, he gave the view-halloo when he saw the redcoats through the raw mist of a winter morning at Princeton and called the affair "an old-fashioned Virginia fox-hunt, gentlemen." His major problem in the war had a still more British flavour. The scanty armies of Great Britain are frequently reduced to a defensive. Indeed, since necessity often compels a British commander to preserve a force which is his country's sole resource, one may almost

term it the national mode of war. Cohesion in retreat and steadiness in prolonged defence are rare
virtues in military history; and in Europe they recur,
more frequently than elsewhere, in British battle-
honours. The trailing march of Moore's exhausted
men across the black hills under the pale skies of a
Spanish winter, until they heard the waves in Co-
runna Bay and turned to fight; the long road from
the piled and tumbled rocks of Beira by way of
Bussaco to the great ridge of hills where the guns
grinned northward in the Lines and Wellington out-
faced the French; the blinding sunlight of a later
summer, by which the left of an Allied line stumbled,
unbeaten, southward toward Paris until it halted
and held along the Marne; these things are in the
direct tradition of British warfare. They seem to
follow in an unvarying succession, by which retreat
is an inevitable prelude of victory. That it is not so
with all fighting nations is clear from one singular
contrast: Mons is an honoured name for Englishmen
but to French ears there is a sinister ring in Moscow.
That, surely, is the military tradition in which Washington lived. He was, before all else, a master of
deft withdrawals and stubborn defence. In other
modes he had, at times, considerable successes. But
they seem somehow less significant of himself than
his central achievement: Trenton may be, in one

view, little more than a neat Colonial raid, and Yorktown was a hammer-blow which owed at least as
much to the anvil of French sea power as to the steady
hammer of the Continental troops. But he did, one
feels, a far greater thing in the long defensive which
maintained an American army in existence from
1777 to 1780. That was the core of Washington's
work as a soldier. Its name, if it needs a name, was
Valley Forge. So perhaps there is truth as well as
courtesy in General Cornwallis' words, when he proposed a toast at dinner in a mixed company by the
York River in 1781 and, addressing his host, observed
that "when the illustrious part that your Excellency
has borne in this long and arduous contest becomes
matter of history, fame will gather your brightest
laurels rather from the banks of the Delaware than
from those of the Chesapeake." Those operations
had been an admirable exercise in the British tradition, with American variants. There was more than
a touch, at times, of the fringed shirt; but the red
coat seemed always visible beneath it. Mr. Walpole
made little learned jokes about *Caius Manlius
Washingtonius Americanus*. But the General was
not a Roman. Perhaps no man was ever Roman
except on his monument. Yet the bad Latin seems
to fling a gleam of light on the tall figure which
stands so still in the shadows. For he was surely of

the stiff company—*Vicecomes* . . . *Armiger* . . .
Comes de . . . —whose images smile disdainfully at
their dog Latin in country churches. He lived in
that grave tradition of good manners; and in it, with
an unwavering finger on his pulse, he gravely died.
At his burial there were three volleys and a salvo of
guns. But, with an informality that must seem
curious in such a case, he never lay in state. The
omission has been abundantly repaired; and it is
his tragedy that his reputation has been lying in
state ever since.

DR. FRANKLIN

*Once in a while I just naturally
sit back and size up this Solid
American Citizen, with a
whale of a lot of satisfaction.*
        BABBITT.

DR. FRANKLIN

THERE is, as all people except inventors delight to say, nothing new under the sun. Under it, a few years back, the embarrassed Agent-General of Mr. Kipling's imagination—"a patient and expostulating person, visibly torn between the pulling Devil of a rampant Colony, and the placid Baker of a largely uninterested England"—discoursed to an exasperated Colonial (since renamed Dominion) Premier those "agent-generalities," which singularly failed to soothe him. And under it, one hundred and forty years earlier, Dr. Franklin, Agent of the provinces of Pennsylvania, New Jersey, Georgia, and Massachusetts Bay, hovered, a somewhat uncertain dove, over the troubled waters of the American question. He found, alas! no rest for the sole of his foot. Ruffled in every feather by the Lords of the Committee for Plantation Affairs, he became almost un-dovelike, perched for a moment on the awful shoulder of Lord Chatham himself; and then, circling warily over the lobby of the House of Lords and Mrs. Howe's in Grafton Street, he headed for home. The flood had not abated. So far as a pair of sharp eyes could observe it from lodgings in Craven Street, Strand, there was nothing in the temper of the King's ministers to encourage a joyous return, olive-branch in hand, across the Atlantic to the labouring ark of Colonial policy. And when the Pennsylvania packet, Captain Osborne, dropped anchor in the Delaware on a May evening in 1775, it brought home a strange emblem of the new national consciousness, aged sixty-nine and with hair that was wearing a little thin now, equally prepared (in the words of a lyric composed for the occasion) to:

> fan the flame which Liberty inspires,
> Or fix the grand conductor, which shall guide
> The tempest back, and 'lectrify their pride,

the Friend, as the poet observed, of his Country and Mankind; but a sad warning to Agents-General. No Agent-General, one feels, should become a national hero. Yet that was the mournful destiny of Dr. Franklin. Perhaps his England was a shade less placid than Mr. Kipling's; perhaps his colony was a thought more rampant. But the problem of that nice adjustment between homeland and colony which, for all his adroitness, he had failed to effect, remained until yesterday. It was left, indeed, for a less logical generation to discover that, for empires as for

Franklin, 1780

From a mezzotint in the British Museum by E. Haid after a portrait by C. N. Cochin

philosophers, the golden rule is that there is no golden rule, that the solution of their problem is that it should be left unsolved.

That failure (or that success) is the tall pillar upon which the friendly little figure of Dr. Franklin was raised to starry eminence. Before it he was merely the sly tradesman with a turn for repartee, who once wrote a sardonic tombstone for

The Body
of
BENJAMIN FRANKLIN,
Printer,
(Like the cover of an old book,
Its contents torn out,
And stript of its lettering and gilding).

But after it he became that universal hero who filled a hundred patriotic perorations, a thousand manuals of self-help; who inspired Lord Brougham to that measured panegyric, which never fails judicial persons upon subjects with which they are imperfectly acquainted; who so pervades a continent that his rapt biographer, observing "few counties in the Union which have not a town named Franklin," has looked closer into the detail of his glory and can exclaim that "few towns of any magnitude . . . do not possess a Franklin street or a Franklin square, a Franklin hotel, a Franklin bank, a Franklin fire-engine, a Franklin lyceum, a Franklin lodge, or a Franklin charitable association." It is a sobering thought, which might well check a retiring man upon the threshold of a career of public usefulness. But Franklin, if he foresaw, persisted; and so became, by his singular achievement, a patron saint of the Republic, a parent added to the grave company of parents, which history had already provided for that gigantic daughter of the West.

Yet this engaging blend of Ulysses and Uncle Ponderevo was remarkably unlike his age. He seems to stray, a little out of place, across the elegant scene of the Eighteenth Century. The lights were lowered; the curtain rose; and as the violins fell silent, a trim garden came to view, in which a gentleman from Philadelphia made a strange appearance. The stout figure, the little jokes, the chuckle, the homespun air contrasted oddly with the formal perfection of the background. Slim gentlemen paraded gravely through life on red heels, absorbed in the solemn business of existing; and Mr. Franklin bustled cheerfully beside them, a sort of universal provider, equally ready to oblige with an Almanac, a printing order, a scientific discovery, or a revolution. It was an age of general accomplishment, when young ladies embroidered with a strange perfection, and even baronets struck the tuneful lyre. Franklin positively

was so far influenced by the prevalence of the Muses as
to confess a sedate familiarity with the harp, the violin,
and the violoncello, and even (with a wilder fancy) to
offer instruction to the mother of Leigh Hunt upon the
more passionate guitar. But competence, one feels,
was probably his mark rather than virtuosity. For
he casts, in that age of artifice, a solid shadow. Even
his piety seemed to belong to an earlier or to a later
time. The sober qualities of the Eighteenth Century,
the sudden interruption of that bright brocade with
broadcloth, must always appear a strange diversion of
the stream. Perhaps they were a throw-back to the
Seventeenth, possibly an anticipation of the Nineteenth Century. At any rate they have far more in
common with either Cromwell or Queen Victoria
than with Mr. Walpole. In this decorous depart-
ment of his time Franklin played a part. It was a
seemly *rôle*, in which he appeared successively as the
thoughtful compositor of Bartholomew Close; the
seeker after truth who presented Mr. J. R. in a
*Dissertation on Liberty and Necessity, Pleasure and
Pain*, with his "Present Thoughts of the General
State of Things in the Universe," listed the virtues
and composed a creed; the respected citizen, dis-
seminating useful knowledge or pouring upon his
fellow townsmen from a capacious cornucopia the
mingled blessings of subscription libraries, street

paving, and fire-brigades; the diplomat in broad-cloth, who walked sedately through the gleaming scene, where France was governed among the gilt and mirrors of Versailles. Seen in this solemn aspect he seems to stand in queer contrast to his age, a wren among peacocks.

Untrue to his time, he was yet amazingly congruous with his place. In an age when minds took little colour from their place of birth and manners were international, when Prussian kings knew little German and Englishmen chopped French and Frenchmen took English airs, Franklin was almost unbelievably American. Even his minor tastes reflected his distant origin. Did not an anxious wife provide a busy Colonial Agent beyond the seas in London with those remote, those unforgettable hickory nuts, dried peaches, cranberries, and Indian meal, which told him of wider skies? Bewildered cooks in Craven Street wrestled with the insoluble problem of buckwheat cakes, like English ministers with the problem of taxation; and friendly hostesses received unexpected gifts of American apples, whilst American nuts were bestowed upon their husbands to provoke thoughts of conciliation over the port, colonial rights being duly safeguarded by the judicious reservation that this tribute was "small indeed, but *voluntary*." Below the surface the whole tone of his mind was un-

European. It had a quality for which it was not easy to find a name in 1770; since the world had not yet learnt to call it American. The poise of his humour; the dry chuckle of "Poor Richard"; the grave, unwinking comedy of the epitaph; the solemn insistence (extended, with a glorious wealth of measured exaggeration, over four years) upon the mythical death of a rival pamphleteer; these things, which seem as personal as the tone of a voice, may all be rediscovered in the later development of his country's comic literature. It may well be his foremost distinction that, politics and electricity apart, Franklin was the father of American humour. Has not a master of that elusive mode detected as its leading form "the humour based on that freedom from traditional ideas and conventional views characteristic of a new country"? By that light American humourists progressed to the clear-eyed simplicity of Hosea Biglow, the calm judgments of untravelled "Innocents," and the inexhaustible enjoyment afforded by protracted horse-trades. And in the first circles of its illumination Franklin sat writing his Almanacs, with his unmoving features and the slow kindling of his amused, his *goguenard* eye. "Poor Richard" is surely the earliest incarnation of "David Harum"; and his creator spoke with the voice which was to come more fully from the lips of "Tom Sawyer," Artemus Ward, and the sweet singer of

John P.
Robinson, he . . .

One catches the note in a dozen aphorisms—in "Three may keep a secret, if two of them are dead," or "Sal laughs at every thing you say, why? because she has fine teeth," in the commercial shrewdness of "Three Removes is as bad as a Fire," or that dispassionate diagnosis of the habit of disputation, "Persons of good sense, I have since observed, seldom fall into it, except lawyers, university men, and men of all sorts that have been bred at Edinborough." Each of his dry jokes is a bold variation upon an old theme, an innovation upon English humour, a Declaration of Independence in miniature.

But there is a more significant particular in which his strange quality as a forerunner of American tendencies is manifest. That patient cultivation of the commercial virtues; those "proverbial sentences, chiefly such as indicated industry and frugality as the means of procuring wealth"; the guide to conduct, which insisted that "no qualities were so likely to make a poor man's fortune as those of probity and integrity"—all this side of Franklin's busy mind must surely introduce him as the first high-priest of the

222

religion of efficiency. The flavour of that modern incense penetrates every happy page of that radiant *Autobiography*, in which he held the mirror up to Samuel Smiles. How true to our own tradition is the ostentatious wheelbarrow of 1730: "To show that I was not above my business, I sometimes brought home the paper I purchased at the stores thro' the streets on a wheelbarrow. Thus being esteem'd an industrious, thriving young man, and paying duly for what I bought, the merchants who imported stationery solicited my custom; others proposed supplying me with books, and I went on swimmingly." That was a wheelbarrow equally, one feels, at home in Philadelphia, the Five Towns, or even Zenith. No Success Editor could pass it by; no correspondence course should omit it. And what modern pen would disdain his judicious advocacy of book-keeping as a feminine accomplishment "likely to be of more use to them and their children, in case of widowhood, than either music or dancing, by preserving them from losses by imposition of crafty men, and enabling them to continue, perhaps, a profitable mercantile house, with establish'd correspondence, till a son is grown up fit to undertake and go on with it, to the lasting advantage and enriching of the family"? That has the authentic contemporary ring of our own preparation for life, of a hundred courses of business training, a thousand handbooks of commercial efficiency.

More modern still (and still more true to his environment) was Franklin's taste for friends in council. Its first seed was sown in the Society of the Free and Easy and in that United Party for Virtue which he longed to form. But its flowering was in the Junto, that delight of Philadelphia Friday evenings, supplemented in the right season by a monthly meeting at "some proper place across the river for bodily exercise." Twelve members wrestled with first principles in debate, explored philosophy, and even turned an attentive eye on physics. But a still closer bond united the philosophers; since a standing question on the club's order-paper enquired "In what manner can the Junto, or any of them, assist you in any of your honourable designs?" The answer, perhaps, lay in that contract for printing forty sheets of the history of the Quakers, which an original member of the Junto procured for the house of Franklin and Meredith. The objects of the club included "the promotion of our particular interests in business by more extensive recommendation," all its members "exerting themselves in recommending business to us." It was the parent-lodge of a stupendous brood; and, across the gulf of time, one acclaims Franklin as the first Rotarian.

His career for forty years was a model of self-improvement, a steady climb up the long hill that leads to affluence. From the days when a small apprentice delivered damp copies of the *New England Courant* up and down Boston to the closing dignity of his long retirement, Franklin pursued an even course. The Muses beckoned; a dozen hobbies tempted; romance was hovering somewhere out of sight; the universe pressed for an answer to its riddle. But the printer's apprentice printed indefatigably on. He served his time at Boston and again at Philadelphia, plying a busy stick and avoiding, so far as possible, in his life (as on the printed page) those "great *errata*," which he notes so patiently. His principles were sometimes queer. When he worked in London, they called him, from his blameless habits, the "Water-American" in the printing-house near Lincoln's Inn Fields, where an alehouse boy was in perpetual attendance and his neighbour at the press required five pints in the course of a normal working day. But Franklin was never a bigot. His austere refusal to subscribe five shillings for the general beer faded before an inexplicable outbreak of misprints in his work "all ascribed to the chapel ghost, which they said ever haunted those not regularly admitted." So he paid, "convinc'd of the folly of being on ill terms with those one is to live

with continually." Equally reasonable was his vege-
tarianism, which finally succumbed to a delicious
bouquet of frying cod on shipboard. The day was
calm; and "it smelt admirably well. I balanc'd
some time between principle and inclination, till I
recollected that, when the fish were opened, I saw
smaller fish taken out of their stomachs; then
thought I, 'If you eat one another, I don't see why
we mayn't eat you.' So I din'd upon cod very
heartily. . . . So convenient a thing it is to be a
reasonable creature, since it enables one to find or make
a reason for everything one has a mind to do."

Once, when in England, he was almost deflected
from his course by the graceful accomplishment of
swimming. He swam from Chelsea to Blackfriars;
enchanted the company by "many feats of activity,
both upon and under water"; and, introducing to
their notice a novel style which aimed "at the graceful and easy as well as the useful," might have become
swimming-master to the sons of a baronet. Perhaps
in Limbo, where Napoleon escapes his fate and is
(as he so nearly was) a British sailor, Franklin in-
structs the nobility in the art of swimming. But he
returned to print; and Philadelphia soon recovered a
busy citizen. At first trade left him with little time
for civic virtue; although in a pamphlet on *The Nature and Necessity of a Paper Currency* he displayed

enthusiasm (natural in a printer) for inflation by a
free use of the printing press. But soon romance had
brushed him with her wing. He knew a glazier with
an absorbing passion for mathematics. The glazier
had a young female relation, "in herself very deserving." Inflamed at length by frequent family suppers,
Franklin demanded her hand and something in the
neighbourhood of one hundred pounds. Her sad-
dened relatives replied that money in such quantities
was not available. But the impetuous suitor sug-
gested that "they might mortgage their house in the
loan-office." His hopes, alas! were unfulfilled. The
bright vision faded; and, after similar experiments
in other directions, the lovesick youth was left with a
sad conviction that "the business of a printer being
generally thought a poor one, I was not to expect
money with a wife, unless with such a one as I
should not otherwise think agreeable." But romance
died hard; and the impulsive printer, remembering
an early love whom he had too lightly left, married
at last.

Business progressed; and he attacked, in spare
moments, the riddle of the universe, evolving a home-
made religion with strictly commercial virtues. Mor-
ality having been rendered unduly difficult by the
wide range of the perfection which it customarily
exacted, he "judg'd it would be well not to distract

my attention by attempting the whole at once, but
to fix it on one of them at a time; and when I should
be master of that, then to proceed to another." He
even evolved a system of moral book-keeping by
double entry, a sort of spiritual audit, which enabled the judicious trader to strike his balances with
the Great Accountant. But gradually he was absorbed in civic life. Public activities crowded upon
his busy imagination, poured in a wild profusion
from the disorderly cornucopia of Daniel Defoe, of
whom he was a zealous reader. Hospitals, meeting-
houses, street lamps, and schools engaged his active
mind. He went from strength to strength, raising
fire companies, reforming the watch, exploring that
paradise of the amateur, the field of education; until
at last, Clerk to the General Assembly of Pennsylvania, he moved in a happy blend of public spirit and
Government contracts. The tedium of debate was
enlivened by the privilege of printing the proceedings,
"and other occasional jobbs for the public, that, on
the whole, were very profitable." At length prosperity, the long pursuit of science, and civic duty,
impelled him to retire from trade; and when he left
the printing-house in middle life, the public claimed
him unresisting.

This singular being made contact at two points
with the life of his time. His trace on its letters,

although he wrote incessantly, was slight. In prose he was merely workmanlike; and the anthologists have shown little favour to his verse, from the heroic manner of his youth,

> Come all you jolly sailors,
>   You are so stout and brave;
> Come hearken and I'll tell you
>   What happened on the wave . . .

in which he celebrated the pirate Blackbeard in broadsheet ballads, to the gnomic perfection of his prime, when he

> governed his passions with absolute sway,

and versified good advice in Almanacs, or even ingeminated in a less tranquil mood,

> Oh! no!
> Not so!
> For honest souls know,
> Friends and a bottle still hear the bell.

But in science and in politics his impact was considerable. From his early inventions (in the patient manner of the White Knight) to his more serious extension of electrical knowledge, his researches disclose the same unpretending busy person who had once hurried about Philadelphia in pursuit of a printing order. It was an age when science had not yet escaped from an agreeable haze of general ideas into the hard light of specialised investigation; and the scientist could still assume the solemn airs appropriate to the pursuit of the philosopher's stone. But Franklin had little taste for deportment; and the long pursuit of knowledge was conducted without false solemnity. Even his electricity was unassuming. The mildest Ajax that ever defied the lightning, he rode sedately on the storm. His work was done without affectation, because it interested him; just as it interested him to devise, when he saw a stove, a better stove; to design, as he passed a lighthouse, a more ingenious lighthouse; to project, whilst he watched the House of Commons, a better ventilated House of Commons.

That busy mind found still more to do in politics. He had learnt in General Braddock's camp, where the redcoats lounged in the spring sunshine of 1755, the mysterious distinction between "your raw American militia" and the King's troops. A queer, distorting mist was slowly rising between the King's Englishmen and his Colonials. First as a leading man in his Province, and later in London, Franklin was sent to grope in it. That his quest for an Anglo-American understanding was, on the whole, sincere is manifest from the positively imperialist ring of his sentiments. Was he not opposed to the restoration of Canada to foreign hands on the strength of a John Bull conviction "that the foundations of the future grandeur and stability of the British Empire lie in America"? He drafted a basis for conciliation with Lord Chatham, no enemy of his country. As the dispute developed, he prescribed "Rules for Reducing a Great Empire to a Small One" with the full bitterness of disappointment; and even when taxation was in the air, when

> We have an old mother that peevish has grown,
> She snubs us like children that scarce walk alone;
> · She forgets we're grown up and have sense of our own,

Franklin could still sing in a loud British voice:

> Know too, ye bad neighbours, who aim to divide
> The sons from the mother, that still she's our pride;
> And if ye attack her we're all of her side,
>   Which nobody can deny, deny,
>   Which nobody can deny.

Deny, alas! they could and did; and some part of the denial was to come from Franklin himself. For his diplomacy in London was hardly equal to the strain; and, in the outcome, events moved faster than argument. Perhaps the absence of the electric telegraph was fatal, or perhaps that majestic movement of British policy—*vera incessu patuit dea*—which made with due deliberation in 1769 the concessions which would, which must have been adequate in 1766, and finally permitted Lord North to introduce his measure of conciliation ten days after a Franco-American alliance had rendered conciliation impossible.

That singular marriage of the young Republic to the French monarchy was the last, and perhaps the greatest, achievement of the old printer. The bride was fair; but, with an experienced bridegroom and no hope of a *dot*, the indomitable matchmaker must sometimes have felt the altar to be almost incredibly distant. The sloop *Reprisal* had run through rough weather from the Delaware to Quiberon Bay in the closing weeks of 1776. They crowded on sail, as the King's cruisers chased the rebel through the November gales. But Dr. Franklin kept below; except when his eternal thirst for knowledge brought him on deck to take the ocean temperature and to verify, by these opportune observations, his opinions upon the Gulf Stream. He was in Paris before New Year, after a brisk encounter with Mr. Gibbon on the road, in which the historian declined to "have any conversation with a revolted subject" and the offended philosopher offered to furnish him with material for composing "the *decline and fall* of the British Empire." The *salons* buzzed with expectation; Madame du Deffand communicated her polite fever to Mr. Walpole; and even at Versailles there was a gentle thrill.

The portent drove in by the mail from Nantes and

descended at lodgings in the Rue de l'Université. The world stared; and how well its stare was rewarded. For, with an uncanny prevision of its demands, Dr. Franklin corresponded in almost every particular with the best contemporary taste. The vogue was all for learning; and here—his spectacles alone proclaimed it—was a philosopher of seventy-two, whom thunderstorms obeyed and learned societies hastened to honour. But he had a higher claim. The world, in 1776, was young and growing younger. It babbled of green fields and played at peasants; it ached for simple virtues; and it adored a noble savage. In an old world turning eagerly back to its own youth the New World was exquisitely modish; and when its ambassador came upon the town in a plain suit and a fur cap, his vogue was electrical. *Le grand Franklin* was made. No classical allusion came amiss; he was Cato, Fabius, Solon, Diogenes, even Pythagoras. Painters and sculptors, engravers and print-sellers put his likeness on every wall, in rings, on snuff-box lids; whilst an angry tyrant beyond the Channel removed his lightning-rods from the Queen's House and sulkily erected some of a rival pattern.

But French policy was still detained by the litigious delights of an ingenious neutrality. Franklin escaped to Passy; and for a year he struggled to elevate Franco-American relations from the dubious plane of gun-running to a more exalted atmosphere of formal alliance. Diplomacy (and the news of Saratoga) prevailed at last. The new Republic had its first ally; and when Dr. Franklin signed the treaty, he wore the suit of Manchester velvet which he had put on in Craven Street five years before for his ordeal in the Committee for Plantation Affairs. For even philosophers are sometimes human. Then came the great day when, unwigged and without a sword, he made his bow to King Louis at Versailles, and Majesty uttered two gracious sentences to the young Republic. The war and Franklin's triumph went slowly on. He saw the Queen at play; he saw Voltaire; he read a paper upon the Aurora Borealis; he listened to innumerable songs in praise of Benjamin and Louis; until at last the gunfire died away, and he set his name to a second treaty. His work was done; and at the end of it all, justly honoured among printers, scientists, Rotarians, and men of letters, he could say with quiet pride that "tho' I did not think that I should ever literally *stand before kings* . . . I have stood before *five*, and even had the honour of sitting down with one, the King of Denmark, to dinner." For he was, more truly than most men of whom it is said, the first American.

234

MR. SAMUEL ADAMS

> *I love my fellow-creatures—I do*
> *all the good I can—*
> *Yet everybody says I'm such a*
> *disagreeable man.*
>
> Princess Ida.

MR. SAMUEL ADAMS

ONE fears sometimes that there can never be an entirely popular Second Chamber in Great Britain, until a judicious constitution adopts the Chamber of Horrors. For this agreeable change must be the prompt and inevitable consequence of any referendum on the subject. Perhaps, indeed, some divination of this stimulating possibility restrained the mellow wisdom of Mr. Asquith from any rash measure of reform in 1911. The public mind, of which we are all a part, is deliciously obsessed by crime in all its alluring varieties. To this flushed vision Dick Turpin represents the national ideal of courtesy towards passing strangers, Charles Peace of patient resource, and Müller of quiet helpfulness to fellow-travellers. For the desperado, whom more squeamish races incline to reprobate, is in our more manly view a national hero. A career of gentlemanly crime leads a hundred actors down the primrose path to public affection; whilst a thousand actresses, blameless in their highest thoughts, patiently counterfeit that *beauté du diable* which makes an irresistible appeal to the Anglo-Saxon imagination. For these depths (especially when of Latin origin) hold an invincible attraction; and, in themselves delectable, they afford exquisite opportunities to overlook, to shake the head in kindly comprehension, to indulge an ecstasy of forgiveness. Such are the blameless cravings of the Anglo-Saxon soul. Is not its favourite exercise the public exhibition of broad-mindedness?

In pursuit of this respectable ambition it makes peculiar pets. Unreadable authors are read with brave determination. Unactable plays are performed with quiet persistence. Art soars superior to perspective, whilst the public taste, determined to enjoy, pants grimly upwards on the thinning air. Poets of uncertain scansion, stung to song by a dyspepsia of thought, are read by a gallant few in limited (but scarcely too limited) editions; and imported sages of intermittent wisdom are sure of a strained, but attentive, hearing, for their tangential messages. It loves, it has made up its mind to love the oddest people; and this determined catholicity of taste even governs its historical admirations. Sedate themselves, these eager worshippers have a peculiar relish for bold defiance of authority by others. Slightly alarming at the time, insurrection acquires a golden glow in retrospect; and the British fancy gazes with mild maternal pride at a long gallery of rebels. Jack Cade and Wat Tyler,

238

Samuel Adams

From an engraving by H. B. Hall after a portrait by Johnston

Pym and Hampden, insurgent Roundheads and even (with reservations due to a more troublesome proximity) acrid Sinn Feiners breathe the soft air of posthumous approval, and "Pretty dears," it murmurs, "naughty little dears," forgiving with the quite unanswerable forgiveness of those perpetually in the right. For rebellion is the surest path to British affections: it is significant that the one member of the royal house to secure universal popularity is Prince Charlie, its only rebel.

We are all rebel-fanciers. In any age our idol has an attractive touch of that endearing furtiveness which makes the heart beat faster. He must cross the stage on tiptoe, and we thrill to see him go. His life is frequently in danger, and he wears the wild charm of outlawry. Often confused with the politician (a humbler class), he should accede to a loftier niche. Superior to the timid company of law-makers, we should enshrine him rather with the more heroic figures which break the law. For rebellion is the sublime of law-breaking.

This artist, since from the nature of his high profession he is bound to live in society, is no less subject than his colleagues to the frequent changes of fashion. He is crop-headed, heavily bearded, and clean-shaven by turns. He affects in a bewildering succession tricolour trousers, red shirts, and Jaeger

239

underwear. He has songs in every key and cockades of every colour in the prism. At the bidding of fashion he discards his Calabrian brigand's hat and assumes a moujik's cap. Brims, peaks, and crowns expand and contract round his head, as the fashion shifts and the eddy of his veering principles dictates. One meets him in togas, in body-armour, in slightly sinister suits of Continental cut, and (in Latin countries) most insinuatingly cloaked. But of all his known varieties the most fascinating to connoisseurs must ever be the revolutionary in broadcloth. It has the piquant charm of contrast, as titillating to the palate as an eloping curate or a burglarious vestryman. In the same taste, for amateurs of crime, a smug incendiary is always the most attractive: for there is something singularly winning in the unusual blend of arson and civics. His bleak exterior affords a delightful offset to the rich rococo of his career. So the unassuming rebel is the drab chrysalis of a gorgeous sedition, the humble envelope which, lit by the accident of history, discloses a skyful of coloured stars—the whole Fourth of July latent in a quiet suit. His sobriety enhances the intoxication; the disorder derives an added charm from his sedateness. For that cause, perhaps, one is irresistibly drawn to that persevering revolutionary who, maintaining a front of inexpugnable rectitude, picked the repressive locks of tyranny and turned against his country that strange instrument of revolution, a Boston town-meeting.

Perhaps (it is not for an untravelled commentator to say) his environment counselled a sober aspect. One cannot imagine that the more flamboyant types of revolutionary would succeed in Boston. Refinement, the child rather than the parent of civilisation, was scarcely yet enthroned in her chosen kingdom. But even before that slightly exclusive dawn, the New England air must always have contained some element unfavourable to indecorum. One can hardly hope to raise riots and Emerson on the same bush; and it is a trifle baffling to picture the cruder forms of insurrection in that well-conducted *milieu*. Other cities may have "known four and twenty leaders of revolt." But their excessive gestures must surely have withered, their extravagant attitudes have frozen embarrassed under that disapproving sky, as their precipitate and unseemly voices died on an unfriendly air.

Yet "this Province," as General Gage was to write ruefully, "began it—I might say this town, for here the arch-rebels formed their scheme long ago." It was an older, rawer Boston. There was a gleam of bayonets in King Street, and Back Bay was almost boisterous. Seafaring men went heavily up cobbled alleys, thumped a familiar table, and called for rum. Ropemakers engaged large-fisted shipyard hands in loud debate, and caulkers aired their hoarse opinions; while more sumptuous figures sat in merchants' houses, magnificent with black silk smallclothes, to say nothing of velvet caps, blue damask gowns, and red morocco slippers. But these splendours and this faint tumult were not the whole of Boston. A more decorous procession trooped, premonitory of later cravings, to Thursday lectures. There was a sober emulation of preachers, a demure comparison of sittings, a modest tournament of texts. Against this background, with its alluring blend of piety and fisticuffs, the Adams family reared an unassuming head. With Devonian and remotely Celtic origins, it conformed exactly to the more austere standards of Boston, where it owned real estate and commanded undeniable respect. The wife assumed the absorbing *rôle* of pietist, while by a pleasing division of labour the husband conducted a malt-house and played a leading part in that ancestor of all caucuses, the Caulkers' Club. Their son displayed an offensive punctuality at school and showed, among other signs of early promise, those mild discourtesies to constituted authority with which later piety customarily adorns the youth of rebels.

But until a full blaze of revolutionary day could fulfil this hopeful dawn, he waited in his corner. Known by the endearing name of "Sam the Maltster," he filled the more modest posts of civic trust, busied himself with public precautions against fire, against smallpox, against defective chimneys; served on numberless committees; even performed without conspicuous success the more distasteful functions of tax-collector. At forty-two he had a misleading air of infirmity. A widower, he had failed in business and lived in a large, unprosperous house. His public life was largely filled by a lingering debate upon his revenue accounts, his thoughts by designs for raising the unpaid arrears. Such melancholy figures are rarely among the more ardent supporters of the governments under which they live. Without a reckless preference for change, they will accept it more readily than their fortunate fellows, since change in their sad careers may always be for the better. Vaguely unsatisfied, they lack the natural conservatism of contented men and are invisibly propelled by their private infelicity towards political platforms, angry deputations, and the scattered musketry of barricades. Modern enquiry, avid of the unconscious, might do worse than estimate its influence in the creation of reformers.

The unprosperous widower in Purchase Street

viewed a depressing world in which Great Britain, just emerged from war, showed an alarming tendency to tax her colonies. Taxation, repellent to all normal beings, was doubly distasteful to a failing trader; and it is not surprising to find him in his first state paper gloomily insisting that "if our Trade is to be curtaild in its most profitable Branches, and Burdens beyond all possible Bearing laid upon that which is sufferd to remain . . . it will be scarce possible for us to earn our Bread." That was an anxious but not yet a disloyal voice. Yet behind his nervous protestations of

the unshaken Loyalty of this Province and this Town—its unrivald Exertions in supporting His Majesty's Government & Rights in this part of his Dominions—its acknowledged Dependence upon & Subordination to Great Brittain and the ready Submission of its Merchants to all just and necessary Regulations of Trade,

there was an awkward undertone which enquired "If our Trade may be taxed, why not our Lands? Why not the Produce of our Lands and everything we possess or make use of? This we apprehend annihilates our Charter Right to govern and tax ourselves. . . . " In 1764, that was not yet sedition. But it might become so; and with an unusual sense of the issue he appended to the Instruction a cautious suggestion that all the Colonies should unite in the appeal against such taxation.

The long debate had opened; and having opened it, the wintry Adams permitted himself a momentary deviation into private life and, with the tempered optimism of a widower, remarried. An anxious woman was added to the anxious family in Purchase Street. But while she contrived for his two children and her baby, he lived the public life. The sober figure, with a greying head and an odd quiver of the hands, moved about Boston. A trifle rusty in his dress (except on the snowy afternoon when he faced the firelight at Governor Hutchinson's in dark red and twenty-eight gentlemen of Council shifted in their chairs), he talked perpetually—in clubs, at street corners, on committees, in Faneuil Hall— except when he was writing in his little study. One seems to catch an echo of him, talking incessantly in a voice that shook a little. Those talks, those endless talks are almost lost. But there was a snatch of them on file at the State House. Mr. Sylvester, inn-keeper, if his sworn information may be believed (and he was, one must confess, a Crown witness), had heard his neighbour, "trembling and in great agitation," exclaiming to a group on a winter morning in '69: "If you are men, behave like men. Let us take up arms immediately, and be free, and seize all the King's officers. We shall have thirty thousand men to join us from the country." The quavering voice persisted bravely—"We will not submit to any tax, nor become slaves. We will take up arms and spend our last drop of blood before the King and Parliament shall impose on us, and settle crown officers in this country to dragoon us . . . first settled by our ancestors . . . free and want no king . . . never better in Rome than when they had no king. . . . " The voice died away, insisting faintly on rights, on power "to give laws to England," on the iniquity of foreign troops, and on the thirty thousand men "with their knapsacks and bayonets fixed," who must infallibly appear from the country at the lighting of a beacon. Harsh, perhaps, and sometimes halting, it was yet a haunting voice. It hung on the air of Boston; and still it comes down the wind, the first voice of the Revolution.

But as yet there was no echo of it in his writings, in those stiff dissertations of "Candidus" and "Vindex" or even in the deeper tones of "Valerius Poplicola," which quoted the classics upon the rights of Governors and citizens and treated English politics with that virtuous detachment which is conferred by geographical remoteness. He could still assure a London correspondent that "all Good Men surely wish for a cordial Harmony between the two

Countrys." He might write gleefully to inform a friend in Charleston that "our young men seem of late very ambitious of making themselves masters of the art MILITARY." But he could assure Dr. Franklin, so late as 1774, that "Britain and the Colonies are considered as distinct Governments under the King": and in the same week Mr. Arthur Lee was informed that his zealous friend wished "for a permanent union with the mother country, but only on the principles of liberty and truth." His voice, one feels, was truer to Mr. Adams than his pen; and that busy, talking voice was echoed wherever a Boston crowd shouted "bloody back" at the harassed redcoats. For if the Revolution dawned in Boston, Mr. Adams was its morning-star.

Later, as the din rose, he found a means to multiply his voice in the Committee of Correspondence. The notion came to him as a means of keeping right-minded colonists in touch with British correspondents—"this is a sudden Thought and drops undigested from my pen." But the plan of enlightening sympathetic Englishmen by post was strangely distorted, when he secured the sanction of a town-meeting for the appointment of a Committee of Correspondence "to state the rights of the colonists . . . and to communicate and publish the same to the several towns and to the world as the sense of this town." The world might listen, if it chose; but in the new design it was, one feels, the several towns that were to be the most interested hearers. So Mr. Adams, raised above his customary crowd in Faneuil Hall, had now an American audience.

The voice quavered implacably on. It debated civil rights with Governor Hutchinson; it informed a hushed Assembly of the detection of certain letters prejudicial to its liberties; it petitioned the King for the removal of their author from the State House. It was a never-ending voice. When the pouting Colonies were wooed in a cloud of tea, it denounced the peril, moved the exclusion of the dangerous herb, announced hollowly that "this meeting can do nothing more to save the country," and raised an echo in the whoop that rang down the empty streets, as the braves made for the harbour in the December moonlight. Soon it was clamouring that "*all* should be united in opposition to this violation of the liberties of all." It was a never-wearied voice, calling endlessly for Congress; a dangerous voice, recognised now in official correspondence as belonging to "the first person that, openly, in any public assembly, declared for absolute independence, and who, from a natural obstinacy of temper, is, perhaps, as well qualified to excite the people to any extravagance in theory or practice as any person in America"; a

248

voice of infinite persuasion in the unaccustomed air of Philadelphia; and at last, as he heard the shots at Lexington, a happy voice. It was the first voice of the Revolution. One seems to catch an echo, with a faint quaver in it.

MR. ALEXANDER HAMILTON

> *No pent-up Utica contracts your*
> *powers,*
> *But the whole boundless continent*
> *is yours.*
>
> EPILOGUE TO CATO.

MR. ALEXANDER HAMILTON

FEW persons, if one excepts the writers of historical plays, have failed to notice the dramatic qualities of history. Indeed, they are occasionally obvious even to dramatists. Sometimes the illusion of the theatre seems to be preserved for whole centuries together; and history becomes a mere welter of "effects." There is a blaze of *tableaux*, a grand succession of *dénouements*, under which the student fumbles unconsciously for his programme. The crowds, the lights, the dresses all persuade us that a curtain has risen, which presently will fall again. The stage is thronged; the minor characters flutter discreetly in their corners. An invisible baton raps sharply in the orchestra; and as the players start and stiffen themselves to swing into a smarter time, the principals stalk to their posts and launch into the grand *aria* or the interminable *tirade*. For Clio quite often has a look of Thespis. Like him, she loves a climax; she has her sudden turns, her grand finales, and (just to complete the resemblance) her *longueurs*. It is all there except the encores. For history, unlike historians, never repeats herself. Each *motif* in the tapestry is rendered once; and as that incomparable pattern winds slowly off the loom, it is nowhere twice the same. Her stage gives only one performance of each episode; and they go by with the perpetual thrill of a continuous first-night.

Sometimes, resolved apparently that one actor shall play his generation off the stage, she seems to concentrate on a single part and leaves a solitary Pope or a lonely Emperor soliloquising before mute, respectful crowds. Quite often she relies on a *raisonneur* and sets some explanatory person like Mr. Pepys or Mr. Walpole to explain the whole piece. But there are moments, especially in revolutions, when her distribution of *rôles* is more profuse. The stage is full of characters, and almost everybody has a line to say. Tyrants oppress and fall; heroic figures strike tremendous attitudes; conspirators conspire; traitors betray; martyrs, conquerors, and citizens cull their appropriate crowns; and whole populations are enlisted in the packed and roaring crowds, whose shifting voices are the ground-bass of the wild concerto. In revolutions there is a part for everyone —a speech for some, for some a hoarse ejaculation, and for some a banner to wave.

Perhaps the strongest need at such times is for talents of a somewhat disorderly character. For that

Alexander Hamilton

From a portrait by J. Trumbull reproduced by permission of the Photographische Gesell-
schaft, Charlottenburg

reason, possibly, Latin races excel and Anglo-Saxons are found a trifle stiff on these occasions. Eminently well-bred, they find with marked distaste that there is so much to do in revolutions which good breeding manifestly forbids. But as the crowds recede, a grateful stillness settles. The departing thunder mutters its way into the distance; decorum silently returns; and as an embarrassed hush falls on the harsh voices of insurrection, there is a call for less exuberant gifts. The revolution has entered on its constitutional phase; and there is a dry rustle of drafts, a clearing of expository throats, as the world prepares to welcome that latest birth of Nature, the new, the perfect Constitution. The last act of a revolution is normally less vivacious than its opening scenes. Decorum reigns, and in an air exhausted of all emotion the new order is hoisted with due solemnity on to its pedestal. A few persons, busy and often a trifle prim, tidy the silent stage, sweep up the broken glass, remove stray small-arms from the blameless scene, and unveil the effigy with those becoming gestures which bring the curtain down. The final tableau demands a sustained expression of public virtue. For that reason, perhaps, Anglo-Saxons excel and Latin races are extremely unreliable in the last acts of revolutions. General Buonaparte, indeed, to whom the *rôle* was once entrusted, ruined the scene completely. Cast to perform the sober office of unveiling the Republic, he scaled the pedestal himself, flourished a sword, displayed his charms before a crowded stage, and made the Empire.

But under British auspices revolutions have less unseemly endings. At home they have closed, to date, in a Presbyterian republic and a Dutch Protestant monarchy. And perhaps the racial aptitude for decorum ordained that the glorious disorder of the Boston streets should die away in the comforting murmur of a Constitution. "We, the people of the United States . . . more perfect union . . . Justice . . . domestic Tranquility . . . Blessings of Liberty . . . this CONSTITUTION." The decent, ritual sound, which admirably becomes the quiet ending of a stormy scene, has almost

the blessed mutter of the mass.

Once more the stage was cleared and the lights discreetly lowered for the last act. Once more a sheeted figure waited on its pedestal to be respectfully unveiled by a small, decorous company. Fiery spirits are rare in such surroundings, which demand a sober quality. It is the chosen moment of precisians, of nicely balanced minds. So it is scarcely surprising that the cord was pulled by the temperate hand of a storekeeper's clerk from a West Indian

sugar island. He may even seem to perform a
humbler office. The piece was ended, and the
packed listeners trooped out into the daylight.
But a busy hand shrouded the rows of empty seats
and left them waiting in the silent theatre for the
next event, wrapped in the incomparable winding-
sheet of the American Constitution. That patient
office must, one feels, have been the *rôle* of Mr.
Hamilton; and the silent interval endured in the vast,
empty playhouse, until they were unwrapped by the
impulsive hand of Mr. Jefferson Davis.

The active little figure seems, at the first glance, too
slight to wear these sober colours to advantage. For
there was nothing in his early promise to forewarn
the world. Others, more prescient, have adjusted
their beginnings to the grave outline of their careers.
For them the White House casts an appropriate
shadow over the log cabin; and a brisk accumulation
of omens enables posterity to display that unvarying
foresight, on which it prides itself. But as he grew
under the blue skies of Nevis, pious ingenuity had
singularly failed to discover the little Federalist
playing significant games in the deep shade. The
father of his country made no sign for years—until,
in fact, the child was born. Even then, indeed, he
wore his paternity lightly. It scarcely seemed to
chill him on that last evening when he sat, leader of

a defeated party, at the long table with the Cincinnati.
Defeated leaders have, in general, a tremendous
solemnity, since they are in mourning for themselves.
But that night he sang them *The Drum*, as he had
often sung before; and Mr. Burr sat staring at him
with an elbow on the table.

The little figure jerked in the West Indian sunshine. Life on a high stool in a small trader's
godown was scarcely stirring. His earliest inclin-
ations were military, and at twelve he aired his
slightly preposterous ambitions to a friend:

"Ned, my ambition is prevalent, so that I contemn the
grovelling condition of a clerk or the like, to which my fortune,
etc., condemns me, and would willingly risk my life, though
not my character, to exalt my station . . . I mean to preface
the way for futurity. . . . My folly makes me ashamed,
and I beg you will conceal it; yet, Neddy, we have seen such
schemes successful when the projector is constant. I shall
conclude saying, I wish there was a war."

It was the mood in which other boys have run away
to sea. Yet it is significant of Hamilton's grim zeal
for self-improvement that when he ran, he sped
(with parental blessings and the warm approval of a
Presbyterian minister) to Princeton. Defeated by a
regulation which seemed to check the pace of his
instruction, he went to King's College. He enters
now the full glare of retrospective prescience which
enabled old gentlemen to recollect the strange prom-

ise of a slight figure seen years before pacing beneath the trees of Batteau Street and muttering to itself; and we breathe at last the true air of heroic biography. In fact, he was a dark-skinned schoolboy, infected with sedition by a few weeks of Boston. At one moment this faithful echo of Mr. Samuel Adams officiated as the darling of a New York meeting, and eager mobsmen greeted the infant prodigy with cries of "a collegian! It is a collegian!" But he declined upon the less exciting medium of pamphleteering.

"I wish," he had confided to his early correspondent, "there was a war"; and at the approach of his desire he joined the Hearts of Oak, who drilled, crossbelted, in green tunics and defied their sovereign sartorially with the bold device *Freedom or Death.* When the war came, he transferred to the less demonstrative arm of the artillery and displayed considerable dash at Brooklyn and White Plains. But, rare among soldiers, he outgrew the schoolboy virtues. Military men, retarded by their splendid calling, often spend a lifetime in their adolescence, thus retaining a Puck-like quality which frequently obstructs their careers as statesmen. But Hamilton was rescued by preferment from this normal risk of his profession. For he was shortly promoted lieutenant-colonel on the staff and became the pen of General Washington. He might contemn the grovelling condition of a clerk; but his clerical talents would not be denied, and he remained a clerk for life.

His clerking was of the noblest order. For four years he ran official errands and drafted inexhaustibly for the Commander-in-Chief. Those plain commands were clothed in becoming prose; General Gates was suitably reproved in person for reluctance to reduce his command after Saratoga; General Putnam was treated still more sharply by the little aide-de-camp; and the sad eyes of Mrs. Arnold watched that slim figure through the dreadful afternoon, when the *Vulture* lay in the Hudson. An elderly colleague named him "the little lion"; and, irked at last by some momentary rebuke, he uttered his little roar. There was a sudden resignation; and, once off the staff, he resumed the schoolboy virtues. Most recent wars have been won by the military impulse of clerks; and, true to his order, he charged through the smoke that drifted on the still autumn air along the crumbling works of Yorktown.

Peace, when it came, did not submerge him, since intellectually he was not a soldier. The toga claimed him; the fine precision of the law engaged his affections; and the little lion roared at juries. But his orderly mind was already attracted by the theme of finance. Few staff officers discuss currency problems with any eagerness; and still fewer currency experts are capable of desiring a national debt as "a powerful cement of our union." That vision, which scarcely troubled the men of the Revolution, haunted him. His elders had drummed out the King; but Hamilton played in the Republic. For his interest was less in the financial organs of the new state than in the State itself. He wrote with exactitude upon a national bank; but his passion was fixed upon the nation, upon "a government with more power" and "an Administration distinct from Congress and in the hands of single men under their orders." For, opening as a rebel, he ended as an empire-builder.

Even before Yorktown *The Continentalist* had lamented that "an extreme jealousy of power is the attendant on all popular revolutions." And in the peace he turned with distaste from "the prospect of a number of petty states with the appearance only of union, jarring, jealous, and perverse, without any determined direction, fluctuating and unhappy at home, weak and insignificant by their dissensions in the eyes of other nations." That glorious riot of freedom might charm republican purists. But it failed to fascinate the young disciplinarian. Perhaps he had learnt a lesson, after all, in the army; and his admiring gaze travelled down a long perspective towards "a great Federal Republic, closely linked in the pursuit of a common interest, tranquil and prosperous at home, respectable abroad."

That note, sustained for seven years in his level intonation, charmed thirteen rebellious colonies into a republic. His mind, unclouded by his own eloquence and unfriendly to the ampler gestures of academic freedom, conceived the United States, withstanding heated imputations of tyranny, of aristocracy, of English leanings and of the grosser forms of personal dishonour. Charges were answered by plain reasoning and chilly rows of figures. The level voice persisted; and this least American of figures, scarcely a father of the Revolution, took the fretful child and made a man of it. For he found a war and left the United States. The note was sustained through busy years of politics, through the grave argument of *The Federalist*, and in the grinding routine of the Treasury. He had contemned the grovelling condition of a clerk. But for six years that sublime clerk sat in the Treasury, founding his bank, consolidating debts, and viewing commerce as an item in the national accounts. One can almost say that the United States were the product of his bookkeeping. It was a singular feat of accountancy; and he performed it—magnificently, irredeemably a clerk. Yet even clerks may sometimes preface the way for futurity. So he kept his word to Ned.

M. DE LA FAYETTE

Beau chevalier, qui partez pour
* la guerre,*
Qu'allez-vous faire
Si loin d'ici ?
  CHANSON DE BARBERINE.

M. DE LA FAYETTE

IT is the essence of chivalry to interfere. The annals of common men are filled with self-regarding entries; minding with nervous concentration their own business, they live their own lives, do their own work, and die in due course their own deaths. But no such unheroic limits are set to the activities of their splendid betters. A fever of altruism propels them into their neighbours' affairs; a passionate unselfishness dictates a lifelong orgy of interference. When they ride out, no dragon engaged in its legitimate avocations is secure from their intrusion, no maiden is permitted to enjoy for long the exquisite agonies of her distress; and drowning men, up for the second time, are exposed to sudden, and frequently distasteful, rescues.

Born far beyond the age of armour and persisting, by a still stranger achievement, into the age of Louis Philippe, M. de La Fayette was all his life an indefatigable member of that busy company. Orphans evoke their highest instincts; stray victims of oppression exasperate them into disinterested, but violent, action; they plunge into protracted adventures on behalf of total strangers tied to trees; and one may be sure, if ever they consent to die for a cause, that it is someone else's. This mood of high endeavour is fed by a continual enquiry into other people's business; and it may be that those flame-pictures of the Hero as Prophet, Priest, and Man of Letters once brushed by a fuliginous lecturer in Albemarle Street, should be supplemented by a portrait, only slightly less engaging, of the Hero as Paul Pry.

This simple craving may, perhaps, account for the unduly high proportion of heroic types produced by Anglo-Saxon races. For they are, as foreign observers almost uniformly attest, incurably inquisitive; and having once enquired into what does not concern them, they have been rarely known to leave it without setting it right. Intrusiveness is the spring of noble actions; and a temper of wholly unwarrantable interference has often earned a statue. Such is, in almost all recorded cases, the mood of chivalry; and it is gratifying to reflect that (in spite of the Latin, almost Gallic derivation of the term) the mood is peculiarly Anglo-Saxon. It is not, one feels, for nothing that the English have selected St. George for adoration: that unprovoked assault on someone else's dragon was irresistible. For what other race

Mᴿ LE MARQUIS DE LA FAYETTE

COMMANDANT GÉNÉRAL

de la Garde Nationale Parisienne

La Fayette, 1791

From a portrait in the British Museum, drawn and engraved by S. C. Miger

has elevated intervention into a foreign policy and raised meddling into a public virtue? Touched with the District Visitor's pleasant consciousness of the deep depravity of other people, they regard the world of foreigners; and a brutal Czar, misgovernment in Naples, atrocities performed upon Bulgarians or Armenians stir a deep response. A strange type of Englishman is even extant which collects foreign grievances as other men collect butterflies. It thrills at the first news of outrage abroad, leaves England in a hurry, and becomes the adopted hero of some foreign land, which honours (but frequently misspells) its benefactor's name.

M. de La Fayette was surely a cousin of that heroic family. Extreme instances of this splendid impulse are Lord Byron, who fought a war upon it, and those accomplished brothers Buxton who, designed by birth to play a leading part in the politics of East Anglia, extended their activity steadily eastwards until it included the entire Balkan Peninsula; whilst Palmerston, who built an active policy upon the same emotion, and Mr. Gladstone, who—more judicious— wrote a pamphlet, are milder cases. A flattering hallucination frequently persuades the benevolent intruders that their devotion is to their victims, that the attraction in the adventure is rather to the maiden than to the dragon. But this delusion rarely

extends to the embarrassed nations which they
befriend. For these kindly foreigners name a street
after them with simple courtesy, and leave them in
total oblivion punctuated by centenaries. But their
saviours glow with an undying consciousness of virtue achieved, of services successfully obtruded, of one
more, yet one more deed of chivalry.

The mood, one feels, is British. Yet once at least
it seems to stand most clearly in a foreign instance;
and, by a pleasing irony, the heroic foreigner intruded upon a British quarrel. When St. George
was French, damsel and dragon were both English.
His country had, indeed, a high tradition of chivalry.
But Bayard seemed a trifle Gothic; crusading attitudes were almost inelegant; and after polite conversation had replaced the tournament, romance was
singularly dead in France. It had sought refuge,
years before, a little further to the south, where
the carved Spanish hills had once watched chivalry
ride out on Rosinante in search of sheep, of wind-
mills, of Maritornes, of the incomparable Dulcinea.
So, when an unromantic Government frowned upon
young gentlemen eager to go campaigning overseas,
they wore disguises, made signs to the inn-keeper's
daughter at St. Jean de Luz, and posted off to Spain.
Somewhere beyond the sunset there was a war; a
brutal tyrant oppressed a virtuous and simple-

minded peasantry; and how could a high-spirited young gentleman in the *Mousquetaires Noirs* do less than fly to the rescue? Elderly ministers might spin tenuous webs of neutrality at Versailles. But where the Spanish hills watch the still waters of Pasajes Bay and tall masts look in at little windows, a sailing-ship of two guns was fitting out in the spring days of 1777; until one morning it moved slowly across the bay, glided between the headlands, dipped to the first Biscayan swell, and left that deep fold of the Spanish hills, with papers (exquisitely misleading) for the Islands and M. de La Fayette on his first crusade.

It is the way of romantic young men to be trans-parent, and the impulsive nobleman was like glass. The Marquis was nineteen; and his motives were luxuriously exposed in an ecstasy of explanatory letters to his wife (he had a wife of seventeen), to his wife's father, to the unsympathetic intelligence of M. de Vergennes. Viewed in a colder light, they have a little of that perfect clarity which, poorly armed and oddly mounted, once clattered through the long shadows of a still summer morning in La Mancha. So the tumbled sky-line of the Spanish hills faded into the east behind him; and, rolling horribly, the *Victoire* crossed the Bay. He felt extremely ill and thought hard of his mission. It was the purest, most untarnishable knight-errantry. Knowing little of the cause, he deeply savoured the adventure. The maid, the lonely tree, the dragon, the single combat danced in his mind; and as they ploughed the *triste plaine* of the North Atlantic, he vowed himself deliciously to the service of his unknown lady, captive beyond the grey seas.

No student of politics, he had heard of the Americans for the first time a few months before. They had declared, it seemed, their independence. Had he not heard an English duke say something to that effect at a dinner-table in the previous summer? It seemed a noble action; and before dinner was over, he had resolved to be their champion. The cause was modish: that season even card-tables proclaimed the superiority of *le boston* to *le whist*. A word (through an interpreter) with Mr. Deane confirmed him; and, indifferent to the finer shades of colonial taxation, but scenting an indisputable adventure, he sailed. If his companions were a trifle mixed, his hopes were high. The sky was bright; he was nineteen; and his crest had recently received the brave addition of a new Latin motto, which challenged grammar and enemies alike with the fierce enquiry *Cur non?* But his reasons were not wholly selfless. Was it not (as he explained to his father-in-law) *une occasion unique de me distinguer et d'apprendre mon métier?* For the young gentleman was a soldier;

270

and eager soldiers often seized such opportunities of active service, before the happy device of autumn manœuvres obviated the professional necessity of foreign enlistment. Yet the motives which urged him westwards into the American service were inalienably French. He wrote eloquently of his *amour pour la gloire et pour la liberté* in an inverted order, of which none of his new friends would have been capable, even if they had admitted *la gloire* to their more austere philosophy. Once, indeed, writing from Valley Forge in the hard winter of '78, he made a more significant admission: *L'abaissement de l'Angleterre, l'avantage de ma patrie, le bonheur de l'humanité qui est intéressée à ce qu'il y ait dans le monde un peuple entièrement libre, tout m'engageait à ne pas quitter.* . . . So the human race was a good third among his motives. The winning places were held by French patriotism and the defeat of England; and America ran last. In the same temper— *persuadé bonnement que nuire à l'Angleterre c'est servir (oserai-je dire c'est venger?) ma patrie*—he wrote a long despatch to Versailles, in which he studied the surest way to ruin England outside the American theatre of war. *Mon amour pour ma patrie me fait considérer avec plaisir sous combien de points du vue les chagrins de famille de l'Angleterre penvent lui être avantageux.* . . . That was not quite the tone of a single-minded friend of the United States, or even of the human race. But it was sound French policy; and in a delighted plan for raids on the British factories in the East he seemed almost to forget the struggling colonists. The distant prospect was bright with disloyal sepoys, jealous nabobs, angry Mahrattas, and sunken East Indiamen; and, with encouragement, M. de La Fayette might have revived the forgotten part of Dupleix. French policy, indeed, which sought its friends impartially among the enemies of England, followed the lead; and after Washington almost its next ally, with a pleasing variety of colour and principles, was Hyder Ali. But it was strange that these sordid calculations should divert M. de La Fayette from his crusade, that he should sully the bright dawn of freedom with worldly thoughts of intrigue among ancient races far to the east: perhaps he wished, like an inverted Canning, to call an Old World into being to redress the balance of the New.

Yet he crusaded on indomitably. The best traditions of knight-errantry were respected by his profound ignorance of the persons whom he was to rescue. Landing in Carolina, he was impressed by the complete equality of rich and poor prevailing in the United States; and, charmed by southern courtesy, he found it grow perceptibly more southern, as he travelled further north. The comments of visitors upon those hospitable States are almost uniformly inane. But M. de La Fayette had come to rescue, not to write the usual book. The maiden was still in chains; the eager knight was at the foot of the tree; and he went off to find the dragon. It was, to be frank, a rather sleepy dragon that the young gentleman and his friends pursued from the Hudson to Yorktown; although once at least he did his best to rouse it to a sense of its position by a challenge to single combat. The bold cartel, delivered to one of His Majesty's commissioners to Congress, evoked the dry response that these national differences could be more conveniently adjusted by the British navy. Baulked of the field of honour, the young Marquis withdrew to his place in the American ranks; but his detestation of *messieurs les Anglais* burned, one feels, with a brighter flame after this gruff denial of the *rôle* of David gloriously matched against a Hanoverian Goliath. Yet his place in the hunt was always prominent. Arriving, aged nineteen, with a vague promise of the rank of Major-General, he found the surprising promise honoured by Congress. Such promotion (for the boy was a captain of cavalry in the French service) was a trifle sudden. But it was due in part to the fact that, singular among the knights-errant whose hearts beat for the American cause, he asked no pay; and, rarer still in the stream of distinguished foreigners which set towards Philadelphia, he was really distinguished. It was sound policy in Congress to hoist the young nephew of M. de Noailles, cousin of the Prince de Poix and son-in-law of the Duc d'Ayen, as a bright standard of French sympathy. So he was given rank and rode on General Washington's staff, an exquisite embarrassment to those French diplomats who were still explaining to Great Britain the strict neutrality of France.

A little gallantry and a wound bravely borne at the Brandywine earned him a command; and he was soon manœuvring colonial riflemen before Gloucester. At twenty he was promoted general of division; and before the year was out, he was of sufficient importance in the army to be moved as a pawn—perhaps a knight—in the jealous game, which a few supple gentlemen in New York were playing against General Washington. But knights are simple-minded; and knightly as ever, M. de La Fayette was loyal to his chief and spoiled the game. He was a bright, engaging figure, in its white French sash and an American general's uniform, which combined delightfully the charms of chivalry with those of an infant prodigy. Whilst a ragged, freezing army cheered "the soldiers' friend," even the British, with their slower perceptions, were becoming gradually aware of "the Boy"; and after the French alliance had almost legitimised his odd position, he acquired a still higher value as a living symbol of the treaty and, almost, as an ambassador of France.

There was a glorious interlude of leave in France, a twelve months' carnival of universal kisses, of respectful ministers, of royal pardon, and sudden promotions. Even the Queen was gracious and begged a regiment of Dragoons for him. He breathed a feverish devotion to his country—*je l'adore, cette patrie.* Once more his guiding motive was visible through the purer flame of his constancy to America: *L'idée de voir l'Angleterre humiliée, écrasée me fait tressaillir de joie.* In this agreeable mood he spent a few weeks on the coast, attached to a force which waited, waited with hopeful eyes fixed on the English Channel. Armies had waited so before, and would wait again. But the Narrow Seas were unresponsive; and the bold invaders never sailed. In this brave endeavour M. de La Fayette was posted further to the west, near Rochefort. He lived in a high fever of expectation of some *grand coup qu'il soit longtemps fera tomber cette grandeur soufflée, cette puissance fantastique.* His task, to be precise, was to emancipate Ireland with his new regiment of Dragoons and a few details of infantry. He had explored the subject, formed (delightful and mysterious process) *quelques relations secrètes;* and the young liberator found the unhappy island *très fatiguée de la tyrannie anglaise.* It was now, as Washington was promptly informed in an eager letter, *le projet de mon cœur . . . de la rendre libre et indépendante comme l'Amérique.* So a new maiden, chained to another tree, gleamed vaguely through the wood; but it was still the same incorrigible dragon.

Yet he was not inconstant. Late in the year he christened an infant son *George Washington,* and sailed for Boston in a cruiser with news of six thousand French troops and a loan. "The Boy" resumed his command, lived through the breathless afternoon at Mrs. Arnold's, and served upon the court-martial which sentenced Major André. Followed a winter interlude of tea and harpsichords at Philadelphia. A lady sang, another played, and there was even dancing. But these timid gaieties ended when the British swept disobligingly into the south; and M. de La Fayette was detached to deal with them. He fenced skilfully with Cornwallis and followed close, as he stumbled heavily towards Yorktown. Later, when the event was known, he wrote with the retrospective foresight common to autobiographers that he had always meant *de repousser lord Cornwallis du côté de la mer, et de l'enlacer dans les rivières*

de manière à ce qu'il ne pût avoir de retraite. That
was not quite, perhaps, the tone of his letters during
the campaign. But strategic insight, rare at any age,
is almost unknown at twenty-three. It is enough
that he played an active part, tired out his enemy,
watched him go to ground by the York River, and
charged happily against his crumbling redoubts in
the last assault. So he could write, a little shrilly,
to Versailles after the unforgettable surrender:
*La pièce est jouée, Monsieur le comte, et le cinquième
acte vient de finir.* For the sleepy dragon was led
captive; the maiden stepped lightly from her tree;
and the happy knight sailed back to Europe, dizzy
with acclamations.

He still, it seemed, had a vague wish to prolong the
adventure. It took the rather schoolboy form of a
craving to appear before King George in American
uniform; and his efforts to obtain a mission for this
spectacular purpose evoked from a sullen English
diplomat an acrid comment on "that vain and
insolent young man." His countrymen, in that
confusion of thought with which allies sometimes
emerge from wars, believed that they had won it; and
the young gentleman was widely celebrated in
France as "the conqueror of Cornwallis," "the
saviour of America with"—generous addition—
"Washington." In the last phase he waited vainly

at Cadiz to sail with an expedition to the Islands. But the quest was over, and once more he roamed the forest, fancy-free.

Inclined at first to vow himself to the service of another, darker maiden, he plagued American states-men with strange suggestions about negro slaves. They stood indubitably in need of a rescuer; and **Mr.** Madison listened politely to his odd confidences upon the topic of abolition, whilst Mr. Adams received a violent denunciation of the crime of slave-owning, "a crime much blacker than any African face." He even made a shy avowal of his views—"*mon rêve favori* (hobby-horse)"—to Washington, announcing that he proposed to purchase a plantation in Cay-enne for the sole purpose of emancipation. In his reply the wise Virginian alluded with grave courtesy to this fresh proof of his young friend's noble quali-ties; he prayed devoutly that his countrymen might one day share the same opinions, but indicated that the possibility was somewhat remote, being convinced that a sudden emancipation would have grave conse-quences, though something gradual might and should be done. The Marquis persevered. But a paler figure shared with the dusky queen his chivalrous affections. For somehow he had become aware that Protestants in France were subject to gross in-justices. By some anomaly surviving from the age of persecution they could not contract legal marriage or even leave valid wills. He burned at this harsh denial of testamentary and matrimonial delights, petitioned ministers, and travelled in the Cevennes in search of Huguenot grievances. Washington was informed beyond the seas of the new adventure and thrilled with his correspondent's detestation of yet another *intolérable despotisme*. But all the while his ears were strained to catch fresh cries for help. The world, in 1786, was exquisitely full of wrongs to right. N. Necker had a new arithmetic; M. de Condorcet had a new penal code; there was even a whole *Encyclopédie* full of new ideas on every topic. Yet he had his disappointments. For sometimes a maiden left off calling just as he had got his lance in rest and spurred at the dragon. Ireland, a promising victim, ceased to need assistance—*tout est apaisé en Irlande, et, de ce côté, il n'y a rien à faire pour la liberté.* Even Holland, which had looked a hopeful case of justice, seemed to fail him: *Je me flattais que la Hollande offrait quelque espérance de ce genre; mais je crains que non.* It is the cry of Quixote. So he roamed the forest, listening hard. But suddenly, quite close to his elbow, he caught a new, a deeper voice. It rose and fell, hung in the air, and rose again; and slaves, Americans, Irish, Dutchmen, and Protestants were all forgotten in his last adventure. For the voice was France.

It thrilled him, when he sat in the Notables, to air his plain American manners and to call bluntly for the States General—*et même mieux que cela.* For France should have a Congress, like his splendid States. It was glorious to scare the Duc d'Harcourt's *salon* by the calm announcement, *Je crois qu'il ferait bien de commencer l'histoire à l'année 1787.* He was twenty-nine that year; and the world had a strange air of springtime. The forest was full of voices, and he rode firmly to the rescue. They called a little timidly at first, in local assemblies, in the long ratiocinations of provincial *cahiers*, in the guarded eloquence of the Constituent. But soon the cry dropped to a deeper note, as the sage gentlemen paced the trim alleys of Versailles between debates and caught upon the wind the big voice of Paris. It swelled and came nearer; and as the smoke drifted across the Bastille, it filled the air, and there were shots in it and cries. A sudden turn lifted M. de La Fayette into power. The free nation formed a National Guard and put him in command. Knight-errantry has rarely ended in a stranger place. He had ridden out as usual, answered the call, and charged with his accustomed fire. The dragon was duly prostrate. But where was the tree, the waiting damsel in distress? Somehow the familiar charm was not working quite correctly. For this time he had rescued a very large maiden from a very small dragon; and she appeared to insist, in breach of all the rules of chivalry, on completing the rescue for herself. Indeed, in the later stages it was not altogether clear which was the maiden and which the dragon. For he found himself assuring a scared monarch that he was *naturellement républicain, mais mes principes eux-mêmes me rendent à présent royaliste.* And soon the dragon abruptly changed places with the maiden, when he came to an open window in the raw cold of an autumn morning at Versailles and knelt to a royal lady in face of a roaring square. This graceful act abundantly fulfilled the exigencies of chivalry. But how far, how strangely the knight had departed from the first objects of his adventure. For it was a distinctly novel experience to rescue a grateful dragon from a bloodthirsty maiden. So he played on his queer, inverted *rôle;* and the name, which had stood for insurrection, became a synonym for bayonets. He could see it plainly now: the French were not Americans after all, and one more historical analogy had failed to work.

Once he retired helpless. He was the Lamartine of '89, without the excuse of being a poet. But they sent him to command an army on the frontier, resolved to confront the enemies of the Revolution with *la constitution et La Fayette*. This specific against invasion was strangely compounded; since the General, no longer a Marquis, fumbled dispiritedly among the northern fortresses, and behind him on the sky he watched the glare of Paris. The place scared him—*lui faisait horreur*—as it throbbed and glowed through the hot summer weeks of 1792; and as his infantry waited, a little hysterically, for the Austrians, he watched over his shoulder. He was still watching, when the streets swept roaring through the Tuileries, splintered a door or so, and saw the Queen put a red cap on her son's head. This ill-mannered anarchy was surely intolerable; and with a sudden impulse he drove south down the white dusty roads, saw once again the glaring city, and faced the cold stare of the Assembly. For those exacting men, whose civic virtues grew daily brighter, disliked the impulses of soldiers. With a movement of chivalry he paid a visit to the lonely Court. But they bowed politely; and, lonelier still, he returned to his army on the frontier. One last adventure seemed to beckon. Might they not bring the King to Compiègne, surround him with loyal troops and give law to France? That last ride—with a smiling Queen, two happy children and a grateful sovereign—would be worthy of any knight. But it never came. So he trailed dismally from camp to camp along that frontier, where the very names—Longwy, Maubeuge, Sedan—were heavy with disaster. *La pièce*, as he had once written from Yorktown, *était jouée*. If any more remained, there was no part for him. Like *Chantecler* he had called the dawn; but when he called again, no sun obeyed him and the sky was unchanged. It was red now over Paris; and in the north, suspected and uncertain, La Fayette was in the saddle with his staff. At last he turned his horse's head towards the frontier and rode, despairing, out of history.

A generation later he made an almost posthumous return. The old man (he was seventy-three) became an emblem of insurrection against Charles X. For he was the past, the free tricoloured past of '89; he exhaled an authentic air of the Rights of Man, the sovereign people, and the *Marseillaise*. So he was swept again down the roaring streets and left, a little shaky, at the Hôtel de Ville. Once more the lance, once more the dragon and the waiting maiden. But this time she was far more manageable; and as the monster withdrew in pardonable surprise to England, she let herself be rescued nicely and stood waiting the liberalism of King Louis Philippe, with grateful eyes and neatly banded hair. The state was saved again; and there was to be—his last historical analogy—an American constitution, where an hereditary Washington should preside eternally over a happy nation. So, for the last time, the knight dismounted, lifted his vizor, took a demure salute, and hung up his armour.

FOOTNOTE ON GREATNESS

FOOTNOTE ON GREATNESS

AND after a few years of writing and a few more of reading one is left wondering, a little sadly, about Great Men. There used to be so many of them. . . . One met them in bronze, in marble, in public speeches, in large octavo volumes, in rather trying epic poems. Some helped to complicate the traffic at congested crossings. Others, more benign, were fitted with drinking-fountains in public parks. But all, whether they leaned on pillars, read from scrolls, controlled incredibly restive chargers with a twitch of bronze reins, or merely served to round off a sentence in someone else's anniversary address, seemed equally to obstruct reflection. A bare mention of them was the invariable signal for a prompt and total cessation of thought, a joyful excuse for all the most riotous forms of intellectual disorder. They were as welcome as a *deus ex machina* to an incompetent dramatist. Tired historians, bowed in enquiry over the causes of events, invoked their names and cheered. Now, the cheer is a friendly sound: but it explains nothing. Citizens, gravely exercised in pursuit of solutions for their public problems, murmured the great names of their party; and the cheers broke out again, swelled to a roar, and stifled thought.   Great Men seemed, somehow, to have become a sort of bromide, a deadly narcotic that arrested all mental processes, sent public speakers straight to their perorations, drugged historical enquiry with a whiff of hero-worship.

There used to be so many of them. . . .   This irritating profusion produced a brisk reaction; and we were promptly favoured with that busy school of biographers, who achieve a precarious distinction by crying down what the world has once cried up. Their method has the faint charm of perversity; and it is, oh! so modern.   But the lampoon has always seemed an ignoble instrument; and what can be more ignoble than a posthumous lampoon?   Besides, if whitewash is an indifferent medium for the portrait-painter, the same is no less true of lamp-black; and in the chilly pursuit of truth (for truth, alas! is the historian's goal) hero-worship by detraction gets one no further than hero-worship by excessive praise.   So one is touched with a mild distaste for our painstaking legion of inverted Carlyles. These ingenious specialists in irreverence are very far, one feels, from the hidden causes.   For you will never explain the riddle of the universe by making noises in church.

There used to be so many of them. . . .   They

stood splendidly erect and looked out so proudly above the silent files of worshippers. But reverence is not always right, and after a few years of writing and a few more of reading one is left wondering about Great Men. Reading was always dangerous to faith; and as one read, one fatally began to doubt. Dubious in the study, the Great Man seems to become still more dubious if one watches him in action. Emerging, as incautious historians sometimes emerge, into contemporary life, one doubts him harder still. The very briefest spell in politics will generally suffice to leave one doubting the greatness of Great Men. For politics in Anglo-Saxon countries abound in Great Men, in figures of superhuman wisdom and prescience almost divine, which issue their opposing (but uniformly inspired) commandments in the competing thunders of their rival Sinais. Men, otherwise sane, will abdicate all judgment in their favour and murmur their names for comfort at grave moments of their country's fortune. These magic effigies command frenzies of enthusiasm, as they confront vast crowds from political platforms. They are made for such spectacular encounters, designed, as it were, to be seen from the front, sculptured in relief rather than in the round. Now reliefs are strikingly unimpressive from behind. That is, perhaps, the reason why a brief course of politics is somehow unfriendly to a burning faith in Great Men. This, one feels at a friendly memory of some familiar figure, is a shrine where demented historians will twirl like dervishes, a name with which orators will calm the fears of multitudes. Here, in an armchair, is the raw material of some splendid myth. For this delightful, inadequate person is an authentic Great Man, bound for the Abbey, safe for Valhalla, sure of his statue and his *cliché*.

So, after a few years of writing and a few more of reading and a spell of politics, one is left wondering about Great Men. There used to be so many of them. . . .

Historians, even married historians, keep queer company. Mild in appearance, they seem to elude those more damaging speculations as to their habitual associates, which assail pugilists and ballet-masters. Yet they keep, beyond all doubt, queer company. Their fellow-men too rarely notice the strange piquancy of those careers, the odd contact of those unassuming figures with their splendid subjects. Meek, suburban scholars rotate habitually with ministers of state; possibly they sustain the tone by the daring expedient of Stendhal's indomitable Marquis, who always changed into Court dress and decorations before writing to Vienna. Retiring persons, who shun the drawing-room at tea-time if stray sounds betray a caller, maintain behind their study doors the oddest familiarity with impassioned blondes of the Renaissance. Blameless (and frequently short-sighted), they bravely parade a professional intimacy with the more pictorial forms of sin; whilst colleagues, only slightly ruffled by research, are on easy terms with Kings. These unimpressive forms walk, unannounced, through palaces, haunt throne-rooms, or sit without invitation at long council tables under painted ceilings; and some, by a supreme absurdity, professing military history, adjust their spectacles and spend half a lifetime in crashing cavalry charges, like those men of letters once evoked by the wicked eye of M. Anatole France plunging, pen behind ear, into the thick of the English arrows beside the Maid.

One may sometimes picture strange encounters of historians with their history. It is delightful to contemplate a mediævalist projected into the Middle Ages or an *amateur* of revolutions adrift in a bread-riot. It is even tempting to set a shadowy scene behind the big windows of the Tuileries under the First Empire, fling back the double doors at the head of the great staircase, and let the liveries bawl the name of Dr. A. (or is it Dr. B.?), to whose unremitting labours all students of the period are irredeemably indebted. One can almost catch the buzz of sudden talk, the quick turn of heads above tall, braided collars, Ney's big laugh and a titter of high-sleeved ladies as M. de Talleyrand, Prince of Benevento and Arch-Chancellor of the Empire, says something cruel behind his hand. Then, in the sudden silence, a drab figure moves uncertainly down the long avenue of watching faces towards the throne where, white-breeched, green-coated, and slashed with a broad, red ribbon, a familiar figure waits.

For some of us a visit to the Second Empire has almost equal terrors. The lights would be so bright, the *Cent-gardes* on the stairs so tall, the music so loud. One could never hope to stroll as airily as M. de Morny, to laugh as loud as Madame de Metternich. But perhaps a sad-eyed lady would smile her fixed Chinese smile; and a head might graciously incline beside her, as the dull eye became almost kind and a slow hand went up to the big moustache.

Only faintly entertaining for the Emperors concerned, such encounters would be highly salutary for the historians. It might amuse their subjects to see the strange, inquisitive caller from the present; and the visit would certainly improve his vision of the past. All realists would be the better for an occasional touch of reality. A modern, just for once in waiting on his Queen, might droop along the tartan wall of Osborne and learn not to patronise his betters. Some lecture-room diplomatist would derive considerable benefit from a silent hour spent sitting in a deep window to watch a still mask bowed above a littered table, where a lean hand wrote long despatches; he might even feel the first uneasy dawn of doubt as to his own prim catalogue of the statesman's motives.

But as the murmur of the anteroom dies beyond the big doors and the little visitor is left with his hero, one is still wondering about Great Men. The past writes steadily at the littered table; the present shuffles uneasily and tries to fathom the tall figure with a star on its coat. And as they sit, one studies the queer contrast and wonders about Great Men. Is the familiar figure (there are statues of him in the square outside, and he gets a chapter in the history books) something quite different from his little student? Is he not a Great Man? Yet greatness is so often a courteous synonym for great success. And success, bright goal of Emperors and correspondence courses, is little more than a chemical compound of man with moment. Combined, they are irresistible. But the man without the moment is as futile as the moment without the man is pathetic, an empty pause in history. Born twenty years before a revolution, Napoleon matured precisely with his moment. The stage was waiting; and he took the centre of it, a Great Man beyond denial. But deprive him of his moment, postpone him by a century, and produce him with identical endowments in 1869. He will reach the age of Montenotte in 1896, may even, if foreign adventure is irresistible, fight in a slouch-hat and a bandolier behind the *laager* of a Boer republic against the riding braves of Dr. Jameson. With a few years of Tonkin and Madagascar to his credit, he will emerge into the sunshine of 1914 in a General's *képi*, stem the German rush, incur republican suspicions, endure the mild exile of eloquent missions to the United States, and die in 1921, a harmless High Commissioner of some mandated territory in the tropics. Such are the mild careers of Great Men who miss their moments.

Our own time has even seen a vivid instance of such failure, a German Emperor who, born two centuries earlier, might have secured his niche. He had the gifts which pass for ability in monarchs; and in an age of monarchy that accomplished mediocrity might have scaled the heights. Those manners, which strike a later generation as merely bad, would have impressed the age of Louis XIV as regal; those parts, which exasperate us by their shabby versatility, must have compelled the awe of courtiers

in the *Grand Siècle;* and in a time of suitable confusion laurels might have crowned that brow, where
an unsympathetic age has set the hat, the unimpressive Homburg hat of exile.

Such speculations leave one with awkward doubts
of greatness. Given a slightly exceptional equipment (and which of us is not exceptional?), is any
man at a great moment a potential Great Man?
Are we all, if the times favour it, ripe for a statue and
a two-volume biography? One drifts more rapidly
towards that uneasy suspicion after a slight study of
the remarkable processes by which Great Men are
manufactured. The primary ingredient is so often
a quite ordinary person. But the pot is stirred by
greater forces; and as the broth swirls round, he
emerges looking strangely different, an unchallenge-
able Great Man.

The normal impetus towards this form of secular
canonisation is national and local pride. The patriot
with his insatiable demand for anniversaries, for
statues, for inspiring examples in all materials and on
every hand is the most prolific creator of Great Men.
After all, a *Sieges-Allee* has got to be filled somehow;
a patriotic banquet must be kept supplied with the
requisite quantity of toasts; art galleries yawn for
suitable representations of the national virtues. The
available supplies of normal men, who figured

honourably at significant moments of national history, are hastily looked over and redressed to play a more impressive part. Memories are ransacked for dim recollections of their early promise. Unsuspected gleams are seen to play about their schooldays. They commonly develop Roman symptoms. With emphatic unanimity they devote themselves to the service of their country, and from these striking beginnings they walk (almost in step) down the long avenue of greatness, where every milestone is an anniversary and the larger landmarks are centenaries. Thus, under the powerful and transforming touch of patriotic mythology, a human being vanishes into the awful draperies of a Great Man.

The transformation is sometimes aided by a more timid class. At moments historians incline to solve their difficulties by attributing unexpected results to personal miracles. A hero is often a rare saving of thought; and one Great Man is sometimes worth a page of economic explanation. This human weakness of our chilly instructors has done something to multiply the pale effigies of the marmoreal Great, which gleam along the path of history. Since they are easy to remember, they are believed to have an educational value; and they afford rare opportunities for a measured eloquence, which frequently reminds the writers of Gibbon. The patriot erects such images as an admirable example to rebellious youth; the historian inclines himself before them, because he often finds that they make an excellent ending for a chapter.

So the strange distortion proceeds with the blessing of Governments and academies. There is a liberal manufacture of Great Men; and their graves, once located with precision, are saluted with impressive salvoes. One little group assists the singular process with rare alacrity—the next-of-kin, who stand with gratified smiles to watch the halo being fitted to a relative's brow, provide the necessary birthplace, relics, reminiscences, and final scene, and do their best to look like him on public occasions. But a more powerful impulse aids these singular apotheoses. The human heart conceals a craving to admire, a rare aptitude for worship. In its higher form this feeling has been shamefully exploited by the most unlikely gods. Improbable deities bask in its sunshine on their unconvincing thrones. But an unexpended surplus of adoration remains available for terrestrial objects, and a large range of human figures is selected for devotional treatment. Custom dictates a uniform glorification of their personal attributes. Their beauty dazzles; their deeds, if they did anything, border upon the miraculous; and the spoken word reflects their unearthly wisdom.

Their life, appearance, mannerisms, tricks of speech, and personal habits are studied with incredible minuteness. Of common men we know little more than the simple fact that they climbed a mountain or saved life from drowning. But of the Great we learn how they pinch sergeants by the ear, fear cats, and take their porridge. In life their slightest tasks and most inconsiderable actions are recorded, after death their most trivial relics are patiently collected; until a grateful world can reconstruct their whole existence from these accumulated *personalia*. This impulse piles the strangest rubbish-heaps round human reputations. Sometimes we may seem in our eagerness for personal *minutiæ*, to honour the Great with a cairn of their cast-off collar-studs. Yet somewhere in these odd proceedings there is a motive. Perhaps the strange desire to reconstruct a selected life in intimate detail conceals a friendly wish to know someone really well. Most intercourse springs from an attempt to pierce the prison walls, to discover what life is like in the next cell; and the source of curiosity about the Great may be the same—with the pretence that they are Great as a polite excuse for the intrusion. Life is a lonely business and most human achievement—art, the family, the tribe, the state, the drama, letters, music—springs from an effort to relieve the solitude.

FOOTNOTE ON GREATNESS

However explained, the detached appreciation of the Great is strangely universal. The true religion of mankind is man. On every hand we are invited to admire unheard-of talents, parts without precedent, gifts beyond parallel. The manufacture proceeds unceasing. The stamp and thunder of its plant is always audible, as it produces with the alarming volume of a great industry; and, like a great industry, it has its strict departments. The hagiologist makes saints; Carlyle makes heroes; the press-agent, with a simpler apparatus for his astrology, makes stars. But the aggregate of these admirations makes, if one may hazard the comment, most indifferent history. For great events have an awkward fashion of being totally independent of Great Men. True history is rarely anthropomorphic. Of the facts that shaped the world we live in, two—the fall of the Roman Empire and the Reformation—are almost anonymous. It is, of course, possible to attach personal labels to them after the event, to find a hero for the play and give him all the choicest lines to speak. But there was no hero in that vague flow of tribes, that incoherent drift of many minds, which made the modern world. Where, looking closer, is the man to take the credit of the French, the American, the Russian Revolution? There were so many of him. He stood about the streets; he stoned the soldiers; he put the leaders up and pulled them down; he died at Valmy, at Saratoga, behind Archangel. He is an elusive hero with far too many names. How much easier to select one figure, cast him in bronze, frame suitable inscriptions, collect his sayings, honour his birthday and make an end of it. Yet even Governments, one feels, must have their moments of uncertainty, when they elbow aside the eager claimants for Valhalla and bury an Unknown Soldier. The wise historian will search history for its Unknown Soldiers. For though there is never, perhaps, a Great Man, there is sometimes a great age.

So one is left still wondering about Great Men. There used to be so many of them. . . .

INDEX

301

INDEX

George III,—*Continued*
funeral, 15–6; other references, 6, 9, 79, 82, 95, 117, 166, 167
Germaine, Lord G., 166–7, 183, 184
Gibbon, 90, 232
Gordon, Lord G., 50, 96
Grenville, 9, 32, 38, 39, 87, 91, 113

Hamilton, youth, 257; ambitions, 258; education, 258; war, 259–60; *Continentalist*, 261; Constitution, 256; finance, 261; *Federalist*, 262; other references, 6, 9
Handel, 16
Hastings, 141–2
Hawke, 153
Henry, P., 10
Hogarth, 16
Howe, 166, 168
Hutchinson, 245

Jay, 48
Johnson, 22, 32, 89, 97
Joseph II., 65–7

La Fayette, opinions, 268–70; American expedition, 269; ambition, 270; hatred of England, 271–2, 275; service, 273–4; Ireland, 275–6; slavery, 278; Huguenots, 278–9; Holland, 279; French Revolution, 280–3; Revolution of 1830, 283–4; other reference, 72
Lee, 165
Lexington, 40, 94, 249
Louis XV., 59, 60
Louis XVI., youth, 58–9; marriage, 59; life, 62–3; America, 69–70; French Revolution, 71–4; death, 73–4

Minorca, 153
Mirabeau, 71

Newcastle, 30
North, ancestry, 80–2; education, 83–4; Parliament, 85–7; opinions, 85; office, 86–7; Prime Minister, 88; India and Canada, 90–1; America, 91–4; war, 94–7; Coalition, 97; old age and death, 98;

other references, 6, 9, 34, 43, 50, 121

Pitt, *vide* Chatham
Pitt, W., 51
Pombal, 27
Pompadour, 59, 61
Pope, 16
Princeton, 208
Putnam, 41, 260

Reynolds, 121, 200
Rockingham, 32, 86, 134

Saratoga, 95, 150, 168
Selwyn, 23
Shelburne, 103, 181

Talleyrand, 71
Tarleton, 184
Thurlow, 89
Ticonderoga, 167
Townshend, 87, 91, 119, 135
Trenton, 209–10
Trianon, 60–4, 71, 73, 74
Turgot, 63, 69

Valley Forge, 210
Vergennes, 63, 67–70
Versailles, Peace of, 234
Voltaire, 11, 234

Wales, Frederick, Prince of, 17–18, 81–3
Walpole, H., 11, 16, 21, 22, 32, 33, 39, 58, 61, 82, 84, 102, 103, 165, 204, 210
Walpole, Sir R., 16, 21, 25, 29
Washington, reputation, 193–8; eighteenth century characteristics, 199–202; as squire, 203; dislike of foreigners, 203–5; French Revolution, 205–6; military qualities, 208–10; death, 211; other references, 6, 8, 9, 41, 168, 260
Wedderburn, 90
Weymouth, 51
White Plains, 187
Wilkes, 33–4, 36, 38, 43, 93

Yorktown, 47, 178, 184–5, 210, 260